AUNT DIGGY'S GUIDE TO RETIREMENT PLANNING FOR CANADIANS

TESTIMONIALS

"Aunt Diggy has a unique way of taking complex retirement and income tax concepts and making them easy to understand. By paying attention to the lessons taught by Aunt Diggy, you should be able to better plan for and enjoy your own retirement."

Jamie Golombek, CA, CPA, CFP, TEP
Vice President, Taxation & Estate Planning,
Aim Funds Management Inc.

"A must read for anyone retired or ever going to retire. Aunt Diggy makes retirement planning easy, understandable and fun."

Talbot Stevens, Author of
"Financial Freedom Without Sacrifice" and
"Dispelling the Myths of Borrowing to Invest"

"Phenomenal! If you liked the 'Wealthy Barber' you will love Aunt Diggy. Once I started to read it I could not put it down. This is a great tool to use with my clients. I can't wait for the next book!"

Eva Heppner, MBA CFP
Certified Financial Planner, London

"In my 20 years of working in the investment industry, I have yet to find a book that can explain retirement planning to this degree of complexity in such an understandable, down to earth and entertaining manner. This is a must read for anyone who takes their retirement seriously."

Lee Corasaniti, CFP
President, Corasaniti Financial Consulting

"Aunt Diggy is a fun and informative approach to financial planning in Canada. It is a must read for the beginner through the advanced as Aunt Diggy helps to clearly explain the many facets of retirement planning!"

Duane W. Green, B.Sc. (*Economics*), FMA, CIM
Vice President, Business Development
Performa Financial Group Ltd.

"Aunt Diggy puts all others to shame! She will entertain & educate you, a definite page turner...enjoy!"

Jenn Killins
Advisor, Mitchell

Published in 2004 by Barry Robert Carson (barrycarson@rogers.com)
63 Atkinson Court (Box 187), Delaware, Ontario, N0L 1E0

First Printing: January 2004

Printer:	Hignell Book Printing (Winnipeg, Manitoba, Canada)
Artist:	Ben Fuller
Editor:	Debbie Shapansky
Text Input:	Caitlin Ellis
Photography:	Victor Aziz
Model:	Carolyn Kingston

Disclaimer: Although every reasonable effort has been made to ensure the accuracy and completeness of this book, the Author and Publisher assume no responsibility for errors and omissions. The information is of a general nature and may not be applicable in your particular situation. Rates and values are approximate and subject to change at any time without notice. Readers must use their own judgement and consult a qualified advisor before taking action. The characters are fictional and any similarities to real people are unintentional and coincidental.

National Library of Canada Cataloguing in Publication

Carson, Barry R., 1962-
Aunt Diggy's guide to retirement planning for Canadians
/ Barry R. Carson.

Includes index.
ISBN 0-9731451-0-2

1. Retirement—Canada—Planning. I. Title.

HG179.C298 2002   332.024'01   C2002-903803-0

CONTACT THE AUTHOR

EMAIL: barrycarson@rogers.com
MAIL: Box 187, Delaware, Ontario N0L1E0

- *Provide feedback on this book or ideas for future publications.*

- *Arrange a no-cost, no-obligation initial meeting to discuss your personal finances.*

- *Order books. Substantial discounts are available for bulk purchases.*

- *Arrange for the author to speak at your group meetings.*

- *Obtain media comments, quotes and interviews.*

- *Receive permission to quote passages.*

CONTENTS

CHARTS

PREFACE

1) *Why do we need another retirement planning book?*

2) *What could possibly be in this book that hasn't already been written?*

3) *What is different about this book that would convince me to read it?*

Aunt Diggy's Guide to Retirement Planning for Canadians is worth the read for the following six reasons:

First, this book is about the retirement planning *process* and not about products. The *process* is much more important! There are numerous books on the shelves that have been written about RRSPs and the many investment products. This book is different. It takes the reader through a step-by-step process for *realistic* retirement planning.

Second, do you have a written retirement plan? Has it been reviewed by a certified financial planner? Would you place your financial well being on the accuracy of your plan? If you answered 'no' to any of these questions, then you must read this book.

Third, I have a *wealth* of hands-on experience (pun intended) dealing directly with *real* people, *real* emotions and *real* life situations. This is not intended to be a textbook dealing with unrealistic people who always do what is financially responsible. We all like to splurge sometimes. I will share the knowledge that I have gained with you. This is a complicated subject but I have put a lot of effort into using easy-to-understand terms and situations that are relevant to the average Canadian.

Fourth, you will enjoy reading the book as I have created realistic, fun characters that you can relate to. Bill is your average fifty-five-year-old Canadian male who wants to know if he can retire at an early age like that guy on TV. You will enjoy joining Bill on his retirement journey. In addition, I have created the Aunt Diggy character. She is a loveable financial planner that provides wisdom and advice. She represents that non-related person in your life to whom you bestow the honourable title Aunt or Uncle. I know you will *love* Aunt Diggy!

Fifth, it will provide answers to the following important questions: Can you retire now? How much will you need? How much will the various income sources provide? What questions do you need to ask? Aunt Diggy will provide the answers and more.

Sixth, don't wait until *after* you retire to find out that you won't get the income you expected. You can avoid unpleasant surprises and learn from the misfortunes of others by reading this book.

Gone are the days of the single income family, where Mom stays at home and Dad works for the same company for life and retires at age sixty-five with a gold watch and a lifetime guaranteed pension.

Those were different times. Today's families must take control and accept responsibility for their retirement. Planning, with the assistance of a trusted financial planner, is the key to success!

I trust that you will enjoy reading this book as much as I passionately enjoyed writing it.

Remember the old adage...

"Nobody plans to fail, they just fail to plan."

BARRY CARSON (aka Aunt Diggy)

ACKNOWLEGEMENTS

Writing a book is no small task and certainly is not an individual effort. There were many friends, family members and colleagues whom I leaned on for encouragement and advice. Without their support this book would have never materialized.

It is not possible to list everyone here but those who helped deserve my sincere appreciation. In particular, I would like to acknowledge the many reviewers who provided valuable input and testimonials, Ben Fuller for his patience in doing the artwork, Debbie Shapansky for her helpful editing input, and Carolyn Kingston for being our Aunt Diggy model.

However, my greatest appreciation and love go to my wife Paula and our three sons: Christopher, Andy and David who gave up precious time with me so I could pursue this project.

DEDICATION

This book is dedicated to my Aunt

Catherine Diana "Diggy" Ferris

1

INTRODUCTION

It is Saturday night, which means Hockey Night in Canada. For years now, Bill and his buddies Brad, Duane and Pete have been getting together at Bill's place to watch the Toronto Maple Leafs.

They have established many traditions. Bill makes his famous chilli, Brad brings his homemade beer, and Pete and Duane just show up and provide a very colourful play-by-play commentary.

Tonight is special because it is Bill's fifty-fifth birthday. Bev has been married to Bill for twenty-eight years and just turned the big five-o or thirty-five American as she likes to call it, as if it were a currency conversion.

The guys were sitting around watching the game and the ladies were in the kitchen, as usual, preparing the food when they overheard Bill say, "I put a lot of work into organizing these nights boys so eat up and enjoy my famous chilli; it isn't everyday you get fine cuisine like this."

The ladies just looked at each other and smiled. They knew they were responsible for doing the majority of the work.

Bev said sarcastically, "Bill's idea of preparing for the evening is to turn on the crock pot and throw in a tin of beans. Oh yes, I almost forgot, he arranges the chairs and makes sure he has the right channel on the TV. Who does he think cleans the house, does the shopping, prepares the ingredients and so on?" The gals just laughed knowing their guys were exactly the same.

Just as the game was getting exciting they paused for a commercial break.

"C'mon," said Duane in a frustrated tone, "how can I comment on the game when they keep cutting to commercials?"

"The Habs (Montreal Canadiens) will kick your butt just like last time, so what does cutting to a commercial have to do with it?" Pete said laughing.

They have the same conversation every time the boys get together but they enjoy this weekly ritual and the friendly rivalry.

Pete pointed at the TV and said, "Look at that guy in the retirement commercial. He doesn't look a day over thirty-five. I don't think he is representative of the average retired guy."

"What a joke," Brad piped in. "Nobody looks that good at retirement. Why don't they show a bunch of guys, like us, sitting in front of the TV enjoying the game? Now that would be a retirement commercial I could relate to."

"I would like to retire someday; I work real hard," said Bill, as he put his feet up on the ottoman watching carefully not to drop the converter. Realizing that he was getting close to retirement age, he asked, "Do any of you guys think you can retire today?"

"I haven't checked my lottery ticket today so ask me tomorrow," Brad said sarcastically.

"No really guys I'm serious for once. What do you think?" said Bill as he put the TV on mute. This was a good indication that this was a serious moment.

Pete alleged, "It is unrealistic to retire at age fifty-five but I know one guy who started working for the railroad at age seventeen and retired at age fifty-two. Financially he was prepared but mentally he wasn't. He is bored out of his skull because all his buddies are still working and he was used to working lots of overtime and didn't have any outside interests."

"You would have to really sacrifice to retire early and the Canada Pension Plan will be bankrupt so let's stop dreaming and get back to the game," Duane commented.

Bill wondered silently to himself if he could retire now that he was fifty-five and even though the guys didn't seem to take the conversation seriously he was no longer focused on the game.

The Leafs and Habs were tied at two goals apiece at the end of the second period and it was time for intermission. The guys went into the kitchen to get a refill on their drinks and visit the ladies.

"Hey there is that commercial again. Bev, come here honey and take a look at this quick!" shouted Bill with a sense of urgency. Bev ran over to the TV to see what all the excitement was about as the TV spokesperson said:

"Yes you can retire into a luxury lifestyle at an early age with careful planning if you call us today for a free initial consultation."

"It's the same couple, but now he is driving to his million dollar beachfront home in his classic mint condition 1957 Chevy," said Pete, shaking his head in disbelief. "If this is retirement, I want some of it," he said laughing all the way to the kitchen.

"Let me put this into terms you boys will understand," said Bev. "You are not even in the same *ballpark* as that guy in the commercial. He is wealthy, handsome and drives a nice car. You guys are just jealous," she said with a smile.

"Hey, I bet I could retire now if I wanted to," said Bill sounding like he was making a challenge to the group.

"Who are you kidding?" joked Bev. "You don't even know how much you need or how much you will get."

Bill thought seriously for a minute and exclaimed, "You're right, I don't know how much I need or even if I am close to retiring now or even ten years from now. I'm certainly going to find out. If the guy on TV can do it, so can I!"

Bev went back to the kitchen. "I think I'm going to faint girls. I just heard Bill actually admit, in front of his friends, that I was right." They all laughed.

Bill had a very serious look on his face. "Seriously guys, do any of you have a retirement plan?" The room was silent for the first time that evening as no one had anything to say. There were no commentaries, no sarcastic remarks, and no expert opinions being expressed. The silence was a historical event in itself. This was the first time Pete and Duane didn't have any words of wisdom to share.

"I'm going to see if I can retire now like that guy on the commercial, now that I am fifty-five years old," said Bill passionately as if he was trying to prove something.

"Hey the game is back on. Now, everyone stop talking about that retirement nonsense. If you really want to retire early, become a hockey player or a coach for the team that doesn't make the playoffs. Now be quiet." Duane was obviously more interested in the outcome of the game.

The next day at breakfast Bev looked directly in Bill's eyes and said, "We should take this retirement planning a little more seriously. We are getting older and I don't know if we will have enough money to retire on. Do you know that I tossed and turned all night just thinking about it and I'm worried?"

"Where do we start?" asked Bill.

"I am not sure, but one thing I do know is that we need some professional advice from someone we can trust. This is not going to be another one of your do-it-yourself projects!" Bill knew exactly what Bev meant referring to the one or two times he didn't think he needed to pay a pro only realizing after the fact that it was going to cost more to fix his handiwork.

"Good luck," said Bill. "I don't want to spend thousands of dollars on a plan from somebody who really doesn't understand what is important to us. That retired guy on TV is totally unrealistic. His lifestyle is not the lifestyle I want. I am not interested in yachts. I am not that type of guy. I just want to maintain my current lifestyle." They both agreed to ask around to see if anyone could point them in the right direction.

Bill asked several of his co-workers about their retirement plans and was very frustrated that nobody could help. He thought to himself, "This subject is very important. Why isn't anyone taking this seriously? Do they just assume the company or the government will take care of them? Perhaps they are waiting until *after* they retire to find out the hard way."

Bev found the same response from her co-workers. In fact, everyone agreed that it was a great idea to have a retirement plan but nobody had actually taken the time to implement one.

There was no shortage of people who had horror stories to share about relatives or people they knew who had worked all their lives and now rely on the government for a monthly cheque. Everyone said how sad it was to watch every penny but Bev got the impression nobody thought it would happen to him or her. She wondered why people were not taking action.

The last person she thought would have a plan was Carlos, a young single guy, but maybe his parents had a plan, so she asked him.

To Bev's amazement, Carlos said, "I do have a plan and it is a good one. I know what I need to save and can party with the rest. *No worry* is my motto."

"What makes you so smart, *young* fella?" said Bev.

"I am no rocket scientist, but I am smart enough to know that Aunt Diggy will take care of me."

"What does your *rich* Aunt Diggy have to do with it? Not everyone is as fortunate as you and some of us actually have to save for our future."

"Aunt Diggy is not my real aunt," Carlos said with a laugh. "She is a certified financial planner. Everyone likes to call her Aunt Diggy. She put together a retirement plan for me and I know how much to save each month to reach my goals."

"Very impressive for such a *young* fella," joked Bev.

Bev rushed home to tell Bill the exciting news. He also had some news to share as he had heard about this Aunt Diggy from Charlie at work. Just like a script on TV, they both blurted, "Aunt Diggy." They broke out laughing.

Bev made the call the next day to book an appointment with Aunt Diggy for the following Monday at Aunt Diggy's office.

SUMMARY OF LEARNING

- Take retirement planning seriously and start planning at an early age.

- Include your spouse and/or other stakeholders in the discussions.

- Retirement planning is not a do-it-yourself project.

- Work with a certified financial planner.

- A plan is only effective if implemented.

NEXT CHAPTER

In chapter two, meet Aunt Diggy and discover what takes place between a certified financial planner and their potential client at the initial meeting.

2

LET'S MEET AUNT DIGGY

"There it is, next to the hardware store," said Bill pointing out the car window to Aunt Diggy's office.

"What a grand old house; converted into an office. It reminds me of the home I grew up in with that long covered porch out front. The gardens are beautiful," said Bev.

"I like the parking right in front. She must park in the back leaving the best spots for clients. I like that," said Bill.

"Look at the welcome sign over the door. I feel like I'm visiting my aunt," said Bev.

"Welcome," said Jenn, Aunt Diggy's assistant. "You must be Bill and Bev. Please have a seat and make yourselves comfortable."

Bill went straight for the comfortable living room style chairs with the padded armrests just like at home.

"May I offer you a drink?" asked Jenn.

"A nice cold glass of water would be great," replied Bill. Bev asked for a black coffee. Jenn wrote their preferences down as a reference for the next visit.

"Wow, they really pay attention to their clients here," said Bill.

Bev pointed to the wall and said, "Look at all those cards."

Jenn brought in their drinks and explained, "They are thank-you cards from Aunt Diggy's clients. She just loves to receive postcards and thank-you cards."

"What are all those photos?" questioned Bev.

"This is Aunt Diggy's extended family as she calls it. Clients are always sending in photos of weddings, births and graduations. This is a group photo from Aunt Diggy's annual family picnic at Springbank Park. Last year there were over one hundred families and we had the greatest time."

"This is the most comfortable office I have ever been in," said Bev. "I don't see a single financial chart. I feel like I've known her for years and we haven't even met."

Aunt Diggy came out and, as expected, had the biggest smile and gave Bev and Bill a very warm greeting.

"Please come in and make yourselves at home." Her office was more like a family room with photos on the wall, comfortable furniture and the warm glow of the fireplace.

"What is that aroma?" said Bill.

"Oh, it should be ready soon," said Aunt Diggy.

"We make fresh homemade raisin and cheese bread. We have an oven in the office so we might as well make use of it. I don't know if my clients come back for the advice or the homemade treats," she joked with a big warm smile.

"Let's get started," said Aunt Diggy getting down to business. "I'd like to tell you a bit about my background and then you can tell me about you. How does that sound?"

"That sounds good. Can you tell me a bit about why you are a financial planner?" asked Bill.

Aunt Diggy explained, "I chose this career because I wanted to make a difference. People were always coming to me for advice on all sorts of things so I figured they must trust me.

"I was working at a fast food restaurant for minimum wage and the only benefit was that I could keep the leftover chicken. I must have five-hundred recipes for chicken: chicken casserole, chicken pie, and chicken soup. I should write a cookbook," she said laughing.

"In all seriousness, my best friend's husband died prematurely at age thirty-eight from a brain tumour and she was left with three young children, no job and no insurance. I wanted to help out but what could I do other than provide moral support and watch the kids while she worked three part-time jobs. I vowed to never let that happen to me or anyone else, so here I am.

"My motto is written on that poster I bought at the mall that reads ...

"Nobody cares how much you know until they know how much you care."

"That is the way I do business. Everyone is family and everyone is treated with respect. I always do what is best for *you*."

"Sounds good to me," said Bev with confidence in her voice. She liked what Aunt Diggy had said.

Bill, in his serious business voice, asked, "What education and training do you have to qualify you to give financial advice?"

"That's a great question Bill. I went back to school to take courses in both insurance and invest-ments. The regulators will not allow anyone to sell these products without having the educational qualifications and licenses. I also continued my education by taking courses in financial planning and obtained my Certified Financial Planner designation that allows me to put the letters CFP after my name. This is an internationally recognized designation requiring successful completion of an approved financial planning program. I must adhere to a strict code of ethics that requires me to take continuing education hours each year to maintain my skills.

"To gain the valuable experience I needed, I started working with a mentor agent named Jack for ten years before branching out on my own. I would like to share a letter that Jack sent to me just before his retirement."

Diggy, experience has proven to me over my thirty-five years that there are TWO simple things that really matter to clients. The first is service and the second is the relationship!

Service must be proactive. Understanding the client well enough to anticipate needs and expectations rather than react when a fire breaks out! Service is meeting with the client regularly to review their plans.

Relationship, on the other hand, is to build trust with clients where I'm viewed as a professional team member. Clients must know how much I care and that I understand their situation.

In building and maintaining relationships I try to have a tailor's approach. He or she always takes new measurements. If we rely on old measurements things won't fit and soon we won't have a client.

While this may all seem very simple and common

in the market place it is not! Finally it's important to understand: one without the other will not work!

"Jack sounds like a very wise and caring man," said Bev sincerely.

"I learned a lot from Jack's advice as he has been a big influence on my success as an advisor. With my twenty years of experience and education I am now qualified to give advice. However, I still continue to upgrade my education as the rules are constantly changing in this business and it is important to be at the top of things. My assistant Jenn has just completed her courses for licensing and is taking on additional responsibilities. She will eventually take over once I retire. It is very important that our clients know we have a succession and backup plan in place."

"I'm impressed," said Bev.

"Let's get down to business. Tell me about you Bill."

"I just turned fifty-five last week. I am a manager down at Carson Manufacturing or CM as we call it. I need some retirement planning advice and you were recommended by Charlie at work."

"Charlie is a real character," joked Aunt Diggy. "He visits just to get the cheese bread."

"What about you Bev?" Aunt Diggy motioned to

Bev that it was her turn.

"I just turned thirty-five American this year."

Aunt Diggy interrupted, "Bill, I see you have a wife with a good sense of humour. We are going to have some fun here. Tell me about your hobbies and your children. I need to know about you before we discuss your personal finances; sort of like dating before we get married," she joked. "Everything that we discuss is confidential."

Bev said very sincerely, "I feel very comfortable. I can see why they call you 'Aunt' Diggy."

They spent the next twenty minutes talking about old times, family, friends and sharing stories. They also talked about Bill's desire to know if he can retire at age fifty-five. It was as if a few old friends had gotten together for a visit to get to know one another again.

"That's it for the first appointment," said Aunt Diggy. "I have a little assignment for you. I want you to make a list of your retirement goals and objectives. I will need to know the age you want to retire and your income need in current dollars before tax. In addition, list things that are important to you. Do you want to retire wealthy or just keep the standard of living you enjoy today? I've seen those retirement commercials on TV and the lifestyle they depict are unrealistic to our clients. There is a financial aspect to retirement but equally important is the mental aspect of preparing for retirement."

Bill looked at Aunt Diggy and said, "You have hit the nail right on the head. Those actors in retirement commercials get your attention but that is not us."

"I would also like to ask you to drop off a copy of your pension booklet or statement, RRSP statements and the most recent notice of assessment for your individual tax returns. This shows your RRSP contribution room. I've been helping people for a long time and if there is one thing I know, it is people," said Aunt Diggy pointing to the hundreds of photos on the walls.

"Jenn will book a second appointment that is convenient for you." She gave each of them a warm handshake good-bye. "Have a great day and remember to tell your family that you love them and give your kids a great big hug. Thanks and I will see you soon."

On the way home Bev reached over and put her arm around Bill. "We found a great person in Aunt Diggy. It is important that we are comfortable with our financial planner and I definitely feel comfortable."

Bill agreed and with anticipation actually said, "I can't wait for our next visit."

SUMMARY OF LEARNING

- Only a certified financial planner can use the designation CFP after their name. This indicates that they have completed a recognized financial planning program and abide by a strict code of ethics.

- It is important to work with a certified financial planner who you can relate to.

- A good client-advisor relationship consists of both service and relationship. The two must exist in harmony as one without the other will eventually result in a severed relationship.

- An advisor should have a backup and succession plan to continue the service to their clients.

NEXT CHAPTER

In chapter three, discover the importance of setting realistic goals and objectives. Learn how to quantify your retirement goals and objectives.

3

SETTING GOALS AND OBJECTIVES

"Good morning Bill and Bev," said Jenn. "May I offer you a cold glass of water Bill and a black coffee for you Bev?"

"Yes, please and I'm impressed that you took the time to record our preference. It shows you care about your clients," answered Bev.

"Aunt Diggy has been looking forward to seeing you today."

Bill thought to himself that she certainly makes you feel like you are her only client and you are very important.

Aunt Diggy came out and gave each of them a friendly Aunt Diggy greeting.

"Are you always this positive and perky?" asked Bev wondering where Aunt Diggy gets the energy.

"All the time. Life is too short to get bothered by little things so just think positively and make the best out of each situation and enjoy life; it could change tomorrow.

"Just look at the World Trade Center disaster. That was a horrific tragedy but have you ever seen so many strangers trying to help one another? They are all so proud of their country and it has resulted in everyone taking a second look at what is important. There is positive in everything but let's not forget those innocent people who lost their lives and the families who are left behind. I hope they had proper insurance and a plan for their finances.

"I have booked two hours today to complete your retirement plan. The first step is to determine how much you will need. Bill, how much do you earn before tax now?"

"I earn about $60,000 a year as the foreman of the plant plus benefits and Bev works part-time as a dental hygienist making about $20,000 a year."

"Do you expect your income to increase?"

"I expect my pay to increase with inflation but I'm at the top pay level for my job so I don't expect much more than the cost of living and Bev will stay the same unless she works more hours and we don't plan on that."

"So you have a combined household income of about $80,000 a year before taxes. Is that correct?"

"Yes," replied Bill.

"I know you have given some thought to how much you will need in retirement, but let me make a few comments before asking for your answer.

Sometimes the final mortgage payment is made and the kids finish school and move out on the day you retire. In this fantasy case, you will suddenly have all sorts of extra money and your income needs will drop. However, in most families the timing isn't quite that predictable."

"I suspect things will be relatively the same in retirement since the house is already paid for and the kids are on their own. We won't have work-related expenses and might need the second car but we plan on staying in the same house," said Bill.

Aunt Diggy explained, "A family will typically need between 60% and 80% of their pre-tax income which works out to $48,000 to $64,000 in your case. Families with significantly affluent incomes usually require less than 60% and families with very low incomes may require a much higher replacement percentage than 80%. The difference between the day before retirement and the day after retirement is important to the planning process. You will no longer have work-related expenses and will not be contributing to your RRSP and pension plan or paying employment insurance. In addition, your income tax bill may be lower. Your lifestyle may not change but your income needs will be less since you don't have all those work-related expenses."

"That sounds reasonable to me," said Bev. Everyone agreed that $50,000 was a nice even number to work with in the plan.

"Step one is complete! Your retirement goal is to have $50,000 in current dollars at age fifty-five before taxes."

"Yes," replied Bev and Bill together.

"There is no right or wrong amount of money to have in retirement but it is so important to discuss things. Sure you can probably live on less but do you want to? A lack of planning can lead to a dismal retirement where you have to watch every penny and life is not fun."

"We agree 100% with you Aunt Diggy. We may not have taken this planning very seriously in the past but we are serious now," said Bev.

"Normally an individual will live between twenty and thirty years after retiring as the average lifespan is age eighty for men and eighty-two for women."

Bill was curious. "Why do women live two years longer than men on average?"

Bev couldn't resist the opportunity. "We get a credit of two years for having to put up with you guys for all these years."

"That is the best explanation I have ever heard," said Aunt Diggy. "Is it ok if I use that with my clients?"

"Absolutely!" said Bev with a big smile.

Aunt Diggy continued by saying, "Let's assume your plan will provide an income until Bill is age ninety even though that is a little longer than the normal life expectancy. I'd rather be conservative because *on average* simply means that half the people die before that age and half live longer so there is a good chance you could live longer."

"Wouldn't eighty-five be a better number to use as it still provides a cushion of three years?" asked Bill.

"Your lovely wife is five years younger than you Bill so when you are ninety she will be eighty-five which leaves a three-year cushion for Bev's life expectancy. With the advances in healthcare I think you will find this is a reasonable assumption to use. Keep in mind that this is just a projection and we can easily modify the assumptions during our annual review of the plan."

"What's next?" asked Bev.

"We use a program on my computer where I input your retirement goals and then we look at the various income sources like the Canada Pension Plan to see how much you are projected to receive. These numbers are compared to your income requirements to determine if you are on track. The difference is quantified so you will know approximately how many additional dollars you will need to save or how much the surplus will be assuming you are ahead of the plan.

"I'll give you a printout for your files and we will review it annually or when circumstances require an additional review. Remember that nothing is guaranteed but I know you will benefit from this process. How does that sound?"

"Just great," said Bill. "Can you do printouts for different ages? For example, can we see a plan for both ages fifty-five and sixty-five?"

"Yes, I will do this plan at both Bill's age fifty-five (Bev fifty) today and when Bill is age sixty-five (Bev sixty). You will see a dramatic difference and I'll cover all the important items you need to know to make an informed decision. Retirement is not something to be taken lightly.

"I've yet to come across a client who complained that they had too much money in retirement, but certainly many are short on the income side. Usually it is due to not getting good advice and failing to plan. Sometimes they just hit an unexpected pothole along the road to retirement. The world has changed. Gone are the days of living off the government in your golden years but the older generation will remind you that this was never the case.

"Sometimes we lose jobs through no fault of our

own or we experience medical problems without proper insurance. I know of several people who were forced into early retirement and they were not prepared emotionally or financially. People come up and comment on how lucky they are not realizing how difficult early retirement can be for certain individuals.

"Have you ever watched the news when somebody loses their house to fire and doesn't have insurance and thought how foolish that is? Most of us have house insurance and wouldn't dream of being without it. What about life, disability and critical illness insurance? What would happen to your retirement plan if you fell off a ladder and couldn't work?"

Bev commented, "I just want to have a worry-free retirement where we don't have to think about the money. I want to be able to sleep at night and keep the lifestyle we have become accustomed to."

"Bill, let's see your assignment. Does it agree with what Bev just said?"

"Yes, I wrote that we want to maintain our current lifestyle and thought we would need an annual income of $50,000."

Aunt Diggy had a big smile on her face obviously pleased that Bill's estimates were in line with her recommendations.

SUMMARY OF LEARNING

- Gather relevant papers like: pension booklets, RRSP statements, insurance policies and a recent tax return. This information is required for your plan.

- A typical retiree needs between 60% and 80% of their pre-tax income in retirement.

- Determine if your lifestyle in retirement will change. A retiree must be prepared both mentally and financially.

- Determine if your income needs will change from the day before retirement to the day after retirement. Quantify the difference.

NEXT CHAPTER

In chapter four, learn how inflation can impact your income requirements over time. Learn what a realistic inflation rate is and the impact of using a lower or higher rate can be.

- 4 -

INFLATION

"Bill, you said your income need is $50,000 a year before tax in today's dollars," said Aunt Diggy.

"That sounds about right," he said, looking over at Bev who nodded in agreement.

"We should spend a few minutes talking about inflation as this can have a dramatic impact on your plan and therefore should be factored in."

Bev commented, "Inflation has been so low recently, do we really need to adjust our plan for it?"

"I'll let you answer that question after we go through a little exercise," explained Aunt Diggy.

"What was your income when you got married and how does that compare to today?" Aunt Diggy asked Bill.

"I made an even $6,000 when I started and have worked my way up to $60,000," he said proudly.

"That would be a tenfold increase over twenty-eight years. Bev, do you remember how much your first house cost and do you have an idea of what it would it be worth today?"

"I sure do. Our first house cost $22,000 in 1976

and I was so worried about the size of the mortgage. That was a lot of money back then and we were not making much. I remember telling Bill that we would never pay off such a huge debt and how I couldn't sleep at night just thinking about it. That same house would be worth about $225,000 today."

"I see where this is headed," explained Bill. "You are going to tell me the amount I need to live off might seem okay today but over time it will be inadequate. We must factor inflation into the plan because if we ignore it we will be sorry down the road."

"Precisely. Bev, did you know your husband was this smart?" said Aunt Diggy sarcastically, knowing that Bill would appreciate that she was just joking.

Aunt Diggy continued to say, "I have heard many horror stories from retirees who were doing okay financially when they started retirement but after twenty years on a fixed income they now have to watch every penny and are forced to give up things that we would consider everyday living expenses, like cable TV.

"We know that inflation can dramatically change your financial situation during retirement and therefore should be included in your plan. Do you agree that inflation must be factored into the plan?"

"Yes, let's include it please," said Bev. "What rate of inflation is reasonable to use?"

"We can't determine exactly what inflation will be but we can look to the past for clues. On the one hand, if we assume a low rate of inflation then you will need to save less money today as the cost of goods and services is projected to be rising at a low rate. However, if the cost of goods and services is higher than we projected, you will be short."

"That sounds like common sense to me," replied Bill.

"Conversely, if we use a higher assumed rate of inflation, then we will need to save more money as the cost of goods and services will be much higher. If future prices are lower than we anticipated, you will have a surplus. Do you really want to sacrifice today to have a surplus in the future?"

"I'd like to project a realistic inflation level so there is neither a deficit nor a surplus. I just want to get close so we don't have any surprises," explained Bill.

"I completely agree with you Bill," replied Aunt Diggy. "The best way to avoid unpleasant surprises is to pick a realistic rate and then review it every year and adjust it accordingly."

"We both agree that we want to use a realistic rate but what do you recommend we use?" asked Bev.

"Let's look at some historical rates so we have a better understanding of what rate should be used in the plan," explained Aunt Diggy.

"The following chart will show that inflation has averaged 3.5% over the past six decades as measured by the Consumer Price Index."

"What is the Consumer Price Index? Is that the same as inflation?" asked Bill.

"The Consumer Price Index (CPI) is a recognized measure of inflation. Assume a typical Canadian consumer purchased a predetermined basket of goods consisting of everyday items like bread, milk, gas, mortgage payments etc. and then determined the cost of that basket today. The same basket of goods is measured at some point in time in the future and the difference is measured. For example, if the basket of goods costs $100 today and $105 a year from today, that is 5% higher. This isn't an exact science but it is one way to measure the average increase in the cost of living. However, keep in mind that your basket of goods could be different than the typical basket of goods, so this is just an indicator.

"The following chart will show inflation over the past six decades with an average increase in the cost of living over that time of about 3.5%.

TIMEFRAME	INFLATION RATE
1990s	2.1%
1980s	6.2%
1970s	7.6%
1960s	2.6%
1950s	2.4%
1940s	4.6%

"These rates demonstrate that inflation is unpredictable and the annual increase in the cost of goods and services could range anywhere from about 2% to 7% over the period of a decade. I would recommend we use a rate of 2% in the plan today," suggested Aunt Diggy.

"Shouldn't we be using a number closer to 3% or 3.5% as that has been the rate historically?" asked Bev.

"Keep in mind that these historical rates include those years where the interest rates were well above 10%. The consumer price index has averaged 2.5% over the past five years and 1.9% over the past ten years. Today, with historically low interest rates, an assumed inflation rate of 2% is reasonable. The important aspect of a plan is to review the numbers each year and adjust for any changes," replied Aunt Diggy.

"Let's see how inflation will impact your income needs over time. The following chart will show how your $50,000 income requirement changes over time using different rates. I have highlighted the 2% column which we will use."

INCOME REQUIREMENTS

Age	0%	2%	3%	4%
55	$50,000	$50,000	$50,000	$50,000
60	$50,000	$55,204	$57,965	$60,833
65	$50,000	$60,950	$67,196	$74,012
70	$50,000	$67,293	$77,898	$90,047
75	$50,000	$74,297	$90,306	$109,556
80	$50,000	$82,030	$104,689	$133,292
85	$50,000	$90,568	$121,363	$162,170
90	$50,000	$99,994	$140,693	$197,304

"I don't think we will need $100,000 or more when we are age ninety. That seems really high to me," said Bill.

"That is what your $50,000 a year will be, assuming a 2% annual increase. At 3% inflation, that same $50,000 income need would grow to $140,000 at age ninety. So you can see how a minor adjustment in the rate can have a very big impact over time.

"Also keep in mind that the annual increase in your basket of goods could be much higher than that of the typical working Canadian. Many seniors disagree with the current rates since their property taxes, healthcare and utility costs have increased at a higher rate. They often read about the 2% increases and question the relevancy given that most of their costs are increasing at a higher rate."

"I see your point," said Bill, "but it still seems like an awful lot of money for a ninety-year-old."

"I bet a $60,000 income and a $225,000 house seemed like a totally unrealistic number to a young man named Bill back in 1974."

"You are certainly right about that," said Bev. "I couldn't have even imagined that our first house would be worth $225,000 and that Bill would make $60,000 back then."

Aunt Diggy suggested, "I would like to use a template showing the income needs at various ages and then we will show the total income from each source and how that compares to the need. We can quantify the shortfall or the excess."

"That sounds like 'a plan' to me," said Bill obviously thinking that his pun was funny.

"The following chart will show the income need for each year between ages fifty-five and sixty-five and then in five-year increments to age ninety. We will use this same template for each source of income and then put it all together to see where you sit at age fifty-five and if you have enough to retire today."

RETIREMENT PLAN TEMPLATE
(*No income sources entered*)

Bill's Age	Income Need	Total Income	% of Need	Shortfall / Surplus
55	$50,000	$0	0%	($50,000)
56	$51,000	$0	0%	($51,000)
57	$52,020	$0	0%	($52,020)
58	$53,060	$0	0%	($53,060)
59	$54,122	$0	0%	($54,122)
60	$55,204	$0	0%	($55,204)
61	$56,308	$0	0%	($56,308)
62	$57,434	$0	0%	($57,434)
63	$58,583	$0	0%	($58,583)
64	$59,755	$0	0%	($59,755)
65	$60,950	$0	0%	($60,950)
70	$67,293	$0	0%	($67,293)
75	$74,297	$0	0%	($74,297)
80	$82,030	$0	0%	($82,030)
85	$90,568	$0	0%	($90,568)
90	$99,994	$0	0%	($99,994)

"In the above example you would be short the equivalent of $50,000 in today's dollars increased at 2% each year. To put this in perspective, you would need a lump sum investment of close to one million dollars."

Bill blurted, "A million dollars! I definitely do not have one million dollars," he said adamantly.

"That number can be a real shocker but if you think of $50,000 a year for thirty years of retirement that adds up to 1.5 million dollars. You require less since your unused principal should generate income. Once we add all the individual sources of income I think you will be surprised at what you learn from doing this exercise."

"I'm certainly interested in finding out so let's get the ball rolling and input the income from the various sources," said Bill anxiously. "I really want to know if we are on track."

"Thanks for providing Jenn with all the information regarding your company and personal savings plans. Before we start with the income sources I'd like to go over the basics of taxation."

"Do we really need to talk about taxation?" moaned Bill, as if he would rather have surgery than talk about taxes.

"Taxation plays a very important role," said Aunt Diggy. "Implementing tax strategies can save you a lot of money. We all should pay our fair share of taxes but no more than that. Do you have any questions at this point?"

"No, I understand exactly what we are doing and so far the visit has been very interesting," said Bill.

SUMMARY OF LEARNING

- A $50,000 income today will be the equivalent to $100,000 income in thirty-five years at 2% inflation and $140,000 in thirty-five years at 3% inflation respectively.

- Your plan must incorporate inflation. A rate between 2% and 3% is realistic today.

- Plans must be reviewed annually and when there is a significant life-changing event; for example, a change in employment.

- Inflation has averaged about 3.5% over the past six decades. It has averaged about 2% over the past ten years.

NEXT CHAPTER

In chapter five, learn why a retirement plan must include a review of taxation basics in order to implement taxation strategies. Learn the five taxation rules that every investor must understand.

5

TAXATION BASICS

Aunt Diggy stated, "Taxation plays a very important role in your plan. I want to discuss the basics as this will assist with our planning later. This will take about ten minutes to review."

Bill moaned, "I don't care about taxes, I just want to pay my fair share and be done with it. Most of these strategies are for the rich, and we average guys don't get any breaks."

Aunt Diggy promised to make this as painless as possible. She handed them both a copy of the basic taxation rates for Ontario individuals.

Taxable Income	Federal Tax	Basic Ontario Tax	Ontario Surtax	Total Marginal Tax
$0 - $32,183	16%	6.05%	0.00%	22.05%
$32,184 - $32,435	22%	6.05%	0.00%	28.05%
$32,436 - $57,111	22%	9.15%	0.00%	31.15%
$57,112 - $64,368	22%	9.15%	1.83%	32.98%
$64,369 - $64,870	26%	9.15%	1.83%	36.98%
$64,871 - $67,289	26%	11.16%	2.23%	39.39%
$67,290 - $104,648	26%	11.16%	6.25%	43.41%
$104,649 +	29%	11.16%	6.25%	46.41%

* As of December 31, 2003

TAX RULE #1: *An individual will pay a higher percentage of tax as their taxable income increases into the next tax bracket. Everyone pays the same rate within the stated tax brackets.*

"Canada has a progressive tax system. This means you pay a higher percentage of income tax at higher levels of taxable income. Looking at the chart, everyone pays the same tax rate on income within each tax bracket. For example, an individual who has a taxable income of $32,184 will pay a rate of tax of 22.05% on their income up to $32,183 and 28.05% on that one additional dollar. The percentage of tax on the last dollar is referred to as the marginal tax rate."

"Hold on a second, I always thought that somebody in a higher tax bracket paid the higher rate on *all* their income," said Bill. "This is the reason a lot of the guys won't work overtime because it ends up costing them more in tax than they earn."

"If that was the case Bill, then somebody who made $1 more could potentially pay hundreds or even thousands of dollars in extra tax and that system simply wouldn't work. I understand how your workers can get confused but their understanding is incorrect."

"Isn't that interesting? Wait until I tell the guys

about this," said Bill shaking his head in disbelief.

"An individual in Ontario who has a taxable income of $20,000 who earns another $100 would pay about $22 in tax. In comparison, an individual with a taxable income of $120,000 who earns another $100 would pay $46 in tax. Does that sound fair?"

"Sure does," said Bill, "because the guy who makes the one hundred grand can afford it!"

"We could spend all day debating the fairness of the tax system but the rules are the rules and we must understand and follow them. There are legitimate ways to minimize the tax you pay if you understand the rules and implement tax-smart investing."

TAX RULE #2: Canadians are taxed as individuals and not as couples. Hence, couples with the same household income could have different tax bills due to this system.

"Equally important is the fact that couples in Ontario are taxed as individuals and not as couples. The significance of this statement should not be understated. It is the foundation for implementing income splitting tax strategies. Let's compare the taxable income of the two couples.

Couple A	Couple B
Spouse 1 $30,000	Spouse 1 $50,000
Spouse 2 $30,000	Spouse 2 $10,000
Total = $60,000	**Total = $60,000**

"Both couples have the same total taxable household of $60,000 in this example. Bev, who should pay more tax?"

Bev looked puzzled wondering why it would be different. "I think they should both pay the same amount as that would be fair."

"What about you Bill, do you want to make a guess?"

"No thanks, I'm sure they pay different rates even though it should be the same."

"The family that has the uneven income levels in different tax brackets will pay more tax. In this case, Couple B will pay more tax than Couple A even though their total household income is the same. (We ignore tax credits etc. for these illustrations.)

Couple A	Income	Tax Rate	Tax Payable
Spouse 1	First $30,000	22.05%	$6,615
Spouse 2	First $30,000	22.05%	$6,615
			$13,230

Couple B	Income	Tax Rate	Tax Payable
Spouse 1	First $32,183	22.05%	$7,096
Spouse 1	Next $252	28.05%	$71
Spouse 1	Next $17,565	31.15%	$5,471
Spouse 2	First $10,000	22.05%	$2,205
			$14,843

"Couple A will pay about $13,230 in tax and Couple B will pay about $14,843 in tax. Couple B pays $1,613 more in tax on the same household income. That is 12% more tax."

"That doesn't sound right," said Bill. "Why would they tax these couples differently?"

"The tax system isn't perfect so it is important to understand the rules. To correct this situation Canada Customs and Revenue Agency (CCRA) established income splitting and legitimate tax strategies to level the playing field. Spousal RRSPs would be an example of this. We will discuss spousal RRSPs a little later when we review your RRSPs."

"This still seems complicated to me," said Bill.

"Let's round the number a little for ease of explanation as it is the concept that is important here to our understanding. The following chart should make things a little clearer but remember these numbers are approximate and subject to change at anytime."

Taxable Income Level	Approximate Tax Rate
First $33,000	22%
Next $33,000	33%
Next $33,000	44%
Everything >$99,000	46%

"Since these numbers are approximate they will serve to illustrate the point as we move through each income source. Keep in mind that any actual tax planning will use the actual current rates."

"That makes it easier for me to understand. We don't need to see the exact rates as long as you are looking at them for us," Bev commented.

TAX RULE #3: Income in different forms is subject to different rates of tax. For example, interest income is taxed at your full marginal tax rate whereas capital gains are taxed at half your marginal tax rate. Dividends from Canadian stocks also get preferential tax treatment. All forms of income within a registered plan are taxed the same.

Aunt Diggy explained, "There is also the principle that all income sources are not treated the-same."

"As long as you are looking after the tax strategies, we are not overly concerned with all the details. If we can save tax we will look for you to make that recommendation," Bev replied.

"What do you mean by all income sources are not treated the same?" Bill asked.

"Interest income and employment income are taxed at your full marginal rate whereas capital gains from the growth of a stock is only taxed at half the gain so effectively you are paying half the rate of tax."

"Why would capital gains be taxed at half the rate of interest income?"

"The government wants to promote investment in companies that provide jobs so they give you an added incentive to do this. In the following chart, an individual earning $60,000 would pay about 33% on their interest income, 17% on income from Canadian dividends and about 16.5% capital gains."

Taxable Income	Interest Income	Capital Gains	Canadian Dividends
$0 - $32,183	22.05%	11.05%	4.49%
$32,184 - $32,435	28.05%	14.03%	11.98%
$32,436 - $57,111	31.15%	15.58%	15.86%
$57,112 - $64,368	32.98%	16.49%	16.86%
$64,369 - $64,870	36.98%	18.49%	23.67%
$64,871 - $67,289	39.39%	19.70%	27.59%
$67,290 - $104,648	43.41%	21.70%	27.59%
$104,649 +	46.41%	23.20%	31.34%

In the above example, Bill would pay $32.98 tax on $100 of interest income but only $16.49 on the same $100 if it is a capital gain.

TAX RULE #4: *Withholding tax is simply a payment toward your estimated tax bill. It is credited to your account with CCRA and is reconciled annually.*

"Withholding tax is another concept that is important to understand," said Aunt Diggy. On your pay they estimate the amount of tax owing and withhold it each pay and remit this amount to CCRA as a credit towards your final tax bill. It is an estimate of what you actually owe. At the end of the year they reconcile and you either have to pay more tax or get a refund. Getting a refund only means you overpaid on your estimated withholding tax."

"I understand," said Bill. "They get you on each pay and then at the end of the year and on everything you buy during the year. I'd rather not even talk about taxes because I pay way too much now."

TAX RULE #5: *Each individual taxpayer is entitled to a basic personal credit equivalent to earning about $8,000 annually tax-free.*

"Every taxpayer can earn up to about $8,000 a year and not pay any tax on that amount," said Aunt Diggy.

"And that's it for taxation for now Bill. There are several other concepts but it is the basics we want to cover here. That wasn't painful was it?"

Bev said, "I actually found that very interesting. I'm curious to know if there are any strategies that will save us tax."

"Well, it is time to start looking at the various income sources to see what you can expect if you retired today."

SUMMARY OF LEARNING

- Canadians are taxed as individuals. Couples who have the same household income may pay a different total tax bill.

- The percentage of tax that you pay for each dollar earned increases as your income increases to the next tax bracket.

- Different forms of income are taxed at different rates. E.g. Interest income is taxed higher than capital gains. All income within a registered plan are taxed the same.

- Withholding tax is simply a payment toward your estimated tax bill. It is remitted during the year and reconciled annually.

- Each individual taxpayer is entitled to an annual basic credit of about $8,000. This is equivalent to earning approximately $8,000 tax-free.

NEXT CHAPTER

In chapter six, discover the income benefit you should expect to receive from the Canada Pension Plan. Are you penalized for taking the payment early? Learn about the Child Rearing Dropout and the Assignment of Benefits.

6

CANADA PENSION PLAN

"The first source of income is the Canada Pension Plan (CPP). How familiar are you with CPP Bill?" asked Aunt Diggy.

"Well I contribute to it off my pay and I've heard it probably won't be around by the time my kids retire. I also read an article in the paper about how some of the money was invested in the stock market and they lost tens of millions of dollars last year. I'll be honest and admit that I'm very concerned that it will run out before I'm finished collecting!"

"Very interesting points. How about you Bev?"

"I share Bill's concerns about the stability of the plan. I also understand that you get *penalized* for taking it early. I just want to know how much we can expect to receive and be able to rely on the payments for the rest of our lives. We really can't afford any surprises if the CPP goes bankrupt. We have paid a lot of money into the plan and I would like to believe we will get our money out."

"Those are very real concerns," said Aunt Diggy. "I can't guarantee the money will be there but I would be absolutely shocked if it wasn't. You see, the majority of Canadians depend on government programs for their daily living expenses and if it ran out the country would be in big trouble. The bigger issue in my mind is that most people do not realize how little they will actually receive from the Canada Pension Plan."

It isn't a question of whether CPP will be there but rather a question of how little it provides.

"Bill, a CPP retirement pension is a monthly benefit paid to people who have contributed to the plan. How much money do you think CPP will provide at age fifty-five?"

"Probably not a lot. I would say about half my need, which would be about $25,000 a year. But hold on a second. If I take it early there will be a penalty so let's say 40% of my income need or about $20,000 a year."

"Interesting; what about you Bev?"

"I think it will be a lot less. Let's say 30% of our need which would be $15,000 a year."

"Bev, do you want to have a friendly little wager with Bill to see who is closer to reality?"

"Sure, if I win he takes me out to that new Portuguese restaurant, Vidalia's Place."

"That place sounds expensive," said Bill. "If I win you will cut the grass for a month."

"Okay, it is a deal." Bev shook Bill's hand.

"Does anyone want to change their answer? This is your one and only chance."

Both Bill and Bev shook their heads confidently indicating that they both thought they were going to win.

Aunt Diggy just laughed and said, "Bev, you should try the codfish as I hear it is excellent. Say hello to Albertino, the owner. He's a good friend of mine and will get you a table by the window so everyone can see how romantic and generous Bill is." Aunt Diggy and Bev laughed. Bill did not find the humour in losing a bet. Not only was he getting a lower benefit, he now had to spend money on a dinner.

"The Canada Pension Plan will provide no benefits at age fifty-five because it is designed to be taken at age sixty-five. You can take it as early as age sixty but your monthly payments will be reduced by 30% as you are receiving five additional years of payments.

"The most CPP will provide is 25% of your income at age sixty-five up to a maximum benefit of $9,615 in the year 2003." (see page 173 for 2004 rates).

"You can't be serious," said Bill. "I don't know if we can afford to go out for dinner now."

Bev nudged Bill which was her way of letting him know that he should stop joking around and get serious.

"Let me explain how the Canada Pension Plan is designed to work. Working Canadians contribute a certain percentage of their income to a maximum amount each year and when they retire they receive a benefit for life based on the amount of contributions. The benefit payments will increase with the cost of living or are "fully indexed" in pension terminology. The working Canadians pay for the retired Canadians who are collecting. However, demographics have changed with the ageing of the population and there are fewer working Canadians to contribute to the plan to support those who have retired.

"You can apply to receive benefits as early as age sixty but the benefit payment will be reduced since you receive more payments. The payments and contributions are based on YMPE which stands for Yearly Maximum Pensionable Earnings and is a yardstick for the average income level. Today it is approximately $40,000 ($39,900 in 2003) so assume the pension benefit will be 25% of $40,000 or about $10,000 a year. In 2004, the maximum benefit is $9,770 a year.

"Hence, somebody making half of the maximum contribution income level ($20,000) would get about one half the benefit ($5,000). However, there is a maximum amount so even though an individual making less than about $40,000 should see up to 25% of their income replaced by Canada Pension Plan. Somebody making more than $40,000 will see a lower income replacement ratio."

"What is an income replacement ratio?" Bill asked.

"The following chart will provide an indication of the percentage of income that could be replaced with CPP at different levels of income. This is the maximum amount at age sixty-five and the average person receives approximately 55% of this maximum amount. The lower amount is due to the individual contributing less than the maximum contribution during the contributory years between ages eighteen and sixty-five.

"Somebody who earns $80,000 will receive the same benefit as somebody earning about $40,000. Clearly higher income earners will get proportionately less of their income replaced by the CPP than lower income earners."

MAXIMUM CPP INCOME REPLACEMENT CHART

Income level	Approximate CPP amount	% of income replaced by CPP
$0	$0	N/A
$10,000	$2,500	25%
$20,000	$5,000	25%
$30,000	$7,500	25%
$40,000	$9,615*	24%
$60,000	$9,615*	16%
$80,000	$9,615*	12%
$160,000	$9,615*	6%

* Denotes the maximum annual CPP benefit for 2003

"That doesn't sound right," said Bill. "If I contribute more to the plan then I should get more out of the plan. Doesn't that sound reasonable?"

"Remember that they both contributed the same maximum amount. An individual earning $80,000 has contributed the same amount as an individual earning $40,000 in any given year.

"It is very important to obtain a copy of your CPP statement from Human Resources Development Canada (HRDC) as the average person gets about half the maximum benefit."

"I don't understand how somebody could get less than the maximum if they earn more than $40,000 a year," said Bill.

"The benefit is based on total contributions from age eighteen until you take the benefit which is usually age sixty-five. The government takes the average earnings, factoring in the increase in inflation, and then determines your benefit based on that."

"I didn't start working until after eighteen because I went to college for two years. Surely they don't count those two years," said Bill.

"The plan is designed to automatically exclude up to 15% of the years in the contributory period, between ages eighteen and sixty-five (up to seven years at age sixty-five) to offset those situations when you were in school or unemployed. Bill, if you look at your statement you have a letter "M" or an asterisk after each year which indicates you contributed the maximum amount and are entitled to the maximum benefit. In the bottom corner it shows your expected benefit and in your case it is the maximum amount. This assumes you continue to contribute at the same average rate and commence benefits at age 65."

"Sounds good to me," said Bill with a smile knowing he would get the maximum amount.

"Here is an interesting statistic from the Canada Pension Plan website which shows the average CPP benefit is a little over $5,200 which is only about half the $9,615 maximum payment. That is why it is so important to get a copy of your statement to avoid any unpleasant surprises. The Canada Pension Plan is also taxable as income each year just like employment income."

Bev showed Aunt Diggy her statement. "I won't even get the half the maximum amount since there were a number of years where I had very little income."

"I bet you stayed home to raise the kids," said Diggy as if to thank her for this effort which often goes overlooked.

"Yes, I felt it was important to their development. It doesn't seem right that I should be penalized for caring for children who grow up to be productive in society."

"How many kids do you have?" asked Aunt Diggy.

"We have two boys and two girls - Carlos, Marcus, Paula and Julie."

"Parents who stay home with the kids are *not* penalized under the Canada Pension Plan if they elect to take the Child Rearing Drop Out provision."

"What the heck is that?" said Bill wondering why the government has to come up with such complicated names for things.

The Child Rearing Drop Out

Aunt Diggy explained, "The Child Rearing Drop Out provision (CRDO) allows either parent to eliminate years with low or zero earning if they stayed home to raise children who are under the age of seven and were born after 1958."

"What does 1958 have to do with anything?" said Bill obviously frustrated with the complications in the program.

"The CPP started in 1966 so you would have to be born after 1958 to be under seven by the time the contributions were tracked. I guess they figure by the time you are seven you don't need the same level of supervision. The key to this program is that you must apply for it.

"One of my clients increased her pension by about $100 a month just for asking and it is retroactive so she also got a lump sum amount on her pension cheque. That extra money can be used for vacations, or perhaps an Education Savings Plan for the grandkids."

"Doesn't the government know I have children?" said Bev in a tone that would suggest she is not impressed with the government.

"It is optional and they don't know if you want to apply this but my guess is that 99% of eligible parents would."

"Why don't they tell you about this? I've been paying for many years and I've never heard of it," said Bill.

"I deal with an HRDC office which is very good at pointing this out to clients who come in, but unfortunately everyone doesn't take the time to come into the office."

"Is there anything else like that we should know about?" asked Bev with keen interest.

"Yes," said Aunt Diggy. "You are also in a position to take advantage of the Assignment of Pension Benefits."

As if scripted, Bill said, "What is an Assignment of Pension Benefits?" shaking his head wondering again why the government makes these things so hard for the average guy to understand.

Assignment of Pension Benefits

"If you recall our discussion of basic taxation you will know that Bill has a higher marginal tax rate than Bev. In your case, if Bev earned $100 she would pay less tax than if Bill earned $100. Since you are taxed as individuals separately and not as couples you have some opportunities for income splitting or tax savings. One of those opportunities is the Assignment. CPP will allow you to split up to 50% of your pension with your spouse. Bill, if your benefit was $10,000, rather than you pay the higher rate on the entire $10,000, you split it with Bev. Bill you still get the same amount as a family but since half your pension goes to Bev and you keep half, the portion that Bev receives will be taxed at a lower rate so overall you save money."

"Sounds very complicated to me," said Bill, "but if I save tax dollars I'm all for it. Sign me up."

Should I commence CPP at age sixty?

"CPP is designed to be taken at age sixty-five but you have the option of taking it at age sixty with a 30% reduction in the benefit.

"The following chart will illustrate this point. Notice that the amount is reduced by 6% for each year you take it before age sixty-five and increased for each year after age sixty-five so the choice is up to you."

CANADA PENSION PLAN 2003

Starting Age	Maximum Monthly Benefit	% of Normal Amount at age 65	Maximum Annual Benefit
60	$561	70%	$6,730
61	$608	76%	$7,307
62	$657	82%	$7,884
63	$705	88%	$8,461
64	$753	94%	$9,038
65	$801	100%	$9,615
66	$849	106%	$10,192
67	$897	112%	$10,769
68	$945	118%	$11,348
69	$994	124%	$11,923
70	$1,042	130%	$12,500

- Pension taken *before* age 65 is *reduced* (by 6% year)
- Pension taken *after* age 65 is *increased* (by 6% year)
- Payable for life and fully indexed for inflation
- Rates are approximate and subject to change without notice
- Check out **www.hrdc-drhc.gc.ca/isp** 1-800 277-9914

"At age sixty-five, the maximum today is $9,615 a year but if you are age sixty you can take it at a 30% reduction so you are entitled to receive a maximum benefit of $6,730. The amount does not go up each year other than inflation."

"Should I take CPP at age sixty or am I being penalized?" asked Bill.

"Yes, you get less but you receive five more years of payments. It is really designed to be equal given that the average lifespan of an individual is somewhere between eighty and eighty-two. I've put together some charts to illustrate the alternatives.

"The first chart just accumulates the payments and looks at the sum. If you commence payments at age sixty-five you will have received nothing during the first ten years of retirement (assuming you retire at age fifty-five) but in the eleventh year your annual amount is much higher than the amount you started to receive at age sixty. Therefore, over time, the higher amounts will slowly catch up. If you live longer than expected, you might be better off waiting until age sixty-five or even age seventy to start collecting."

CANADA PENSION PLAN 2003
Total Accumulated Dollars
0% interest 2% inflation

AGE	Start at AGE 60	Start at AGE 65	Start at AGE 70
60	$6,732	$0	$0
61	$13,599	$0	$0
62	$20,603	$0	$0
63	$27,747	$0	$0
64	$35,034	$0	$0
65	$42,466	$10,780	$0
70	$81,920	$73,183	$15,240
75	$125,480	$129,086	$78,877
80	$173,573	$212,218	$152,158
85	$226,673	$289,588	$233,066

- Payments will increase with interest (chart assumes zero interest for simplicity)
- The extra value of receiving money early has not been factored in
- Assumes 2% inflation rate

"The highlighted areas show the higher total payments at each age. For example, if you died in your sixtieth year, you would be better off commencing the payment at age sixty versus waiting until age sixty-five.

"The second chart is more realistic as it factors in that $1 received today is better than $1 received tomorrow. Assuming a 5% return, you can see that the typical pensioner is no worse off for taking CPP at sixty. That dispels the myth that you are penalized for taking CPP at age sixty."

CANADA PENSION PLAN 2003
AGE COMPARISON:
Cumulative Dollars Invested @ 5%

AGE	Start at AGE 60	Start at AGE 65	Start at AGE 70
60	$6,913	$0	$0
61	$14,310	$0	$0
62	$22,218	$0	$0
63	$30,665	$0	$0
64	$39,681	$0	$0
65	$49,297	$10,893	$0
70	$107,604	$77,680	$15,650
75	$186,671	$169,557	$111,600
80	$292,717	$294,148	$243,595
85	$433,732	$461,251	$422,588

- Payments will increase with inflation (chart assumes zero inflation for simplicity)
- The extra value of receiving money early has been factored in @ 5%

Aunt Diggy explained, "The breakeven point is somewhere between ages seventy-five and eighty which just happens to correspond with the average lifespan. Let's fill in the chart and see where you would be with just CPP. Remember that the amounts

Bill's Age	Income Need	CPP Bill	CPP Bev	Total Income
55	$50,000	$0	$0	$0
56	$51,000	$0	$0	$0
57	$52,020	$0	$0	$0
58	$53,060	$0	$0	$0
59	$54,122	$0	$0	$0
60	$55,204	$7,431	$0	$7,431
61	$56,308	$7,580	$0	$7,580
62	$57,434	$7,731	$0	$7,731
63	$58,583	$7,886	$0	$7,886
64	$59,755	$8,044	$0	$8,044
65	$60,950	$8,204	$4,102	$12,306
70	$67,293	$9,058	$4,529	$13,587
75	$74,297	$10,001	$5,000	$15,001
80	$82,030	$11,042	$5,521	$16,563
85	$90,568	$12,191	$6,096	$18,287
90	$99,994	$13,460	$6,730	$20,190

will be higher due to the assumed 2% annual increase in the payments due to inflation."

"It isn't my intention to scare you but the reality is that retirement at age fifty-five is unrealistic if you rely solely on CPP. You can clearly see that CPP will not fund your retirement to the degree you expected.

"At age sixty-five it will only provide about twenty percent of your need."

"I had no idea. How do people retire at age fifty-five?" asked Bill.

"It takes planning, realistic expectations and some degree of saving today for benefit tomorrow. The majority of people I know that retire at fifty-five have wonderful pension plans at work and have long tenure with that particular company, such as police officers. The key is to know what to expect to see if you are on track and what it is going to take.

"The first chart is a snapshot at age fifty-five with only CPP. The chart will show your Income Need, Total Income received from the sources included, the percentage of your need met, and the shortfall or surplus in dollars. We will go through each source and build on this until we have a complete snapshot of your situation today at age fifty-five."

INCOME AT AGE 55
(CPP ONLY)

Bill's Age	Income Need	Total Income	% of Need	Shortfall / Surplus
55	$50,000	$0	0%	($50,000)
56	$51,000	$0	0%	($51,000)
57	$52,020	$0	0%	($52,020)
58	$53,060	$0	0%	($53,060)
59	$54,122	$0	0%	($54,122)
60	$55,204	$7,431	13%	($47,773)
61	$56,308	$7,580	13%	($48,728)
62	$57,434	$7,731	13%	($49,703)
63	$58,583	$7,886	13%	($50,697)
64	$59,755	$8,044	13%	($51,711)
65	$60,950	$12,306	20%	($48,644)
70	$67,293	$13,587	20%	($53,706)
75	$74,297	$15,001	20%	($59,296)
80	$82,030	$16,563	20%	($65,467)
85	$90,568	$18,287	20%	($72,281)
90	$99,994	$20,190	20%	($79,804)

"This chart demonstrates that the CPP will not provide any income between ages fifty-five and sixty and then only about 13% of the need. You can wait until age sixty-five to commence CPP but then the income need met would be zero percent.

"Let's look at the total income projection at age fifty-five and then quickly change the numbers to see what the numbers look like at age sixty-five using this planning software that I have."

"Sounds good to me," said Bev.

"I can't believe how little we get," said Bill.

Diggy replied, "It is much better to know on paper now than after you retire and be surprised. It is really designed to provide a basic income at age sixty-five so you must rely on other sources of retirement income. Are you both surprised at the results?"

"Absolutely," said Bev. "I was so worried about it not being there but I had no idea how little you actually get and in particular at age fifty-five and sixty.

"They should call it the Income *Insecurity* program," griped Bill.

"But that isn't the only source of income. HRDC also administers the Old Age Security program (OAS). Let's look at that next," said Aunt Diggy.

"I'm still concerned about it not being there," said Bev.

"Contribution level will increase and the rules for collecting the benefits might change but I am confident the program will continue.

"Here is a brochure you can read. All the forms you will need to apply for benefits, if you still need them, are available at your local HRDC office."

"It has been very interesting. How do you learn all this stuff?" Bill asked.

"Well, unfortunately I have learned by the mistakes of others who didn't know the rules. Imagine the surprise when you retire at age fifty-five and learn you don't get the full CPP benefits until age sixty-five?"

"Well I have mixed emotions about seeing the final results. I have a feeling there will not be enough money to retire this year or next but I am also anxious to find out," replied Bill.

"In the next hour you will know how realistic retirement is at your age of fifty-five and how that compares to say age sixty-five. In addition, you will know the answers to all the key questions you should be asking. It is so important to know this information but many Canadians simply stick their head in the sand and assume they will be okay. Remember the old adage...

"Nobody plans to fail they just fail to plan."

Bev and Bill agreed. "The kids could really benefit from this advice. They don't have a lot of money but would you help them out?" asked Bev.

"Absolutely," said Diggy, "I'll call them this week; it is important that they know this information when they are young. Let's now take a look at the other government income security program called Old Age Security or as Bill would call it Old Age Insecurity," she joked.

SUMMARY OF LEARNING

- CPP can commence as early as age sixty and as late as age seventy. It is reduced by 6% for each year prior to age sixty-five and increased by 6% for each year after age sixty-five.

- Current maximum annual benefit payment for 2004 is $9,770 ($814 monthly).

- CPP is designed to replace 25% of income up to income levels of $40,000. Someone earning $80,000 has the same benefit as somebody earning $40,000.

- The Child Rearing Drop Out adjusts the benefit for parents who stayed at home with young children.

- Spouses can share CPP benefits to take advantage of income splitting.

NEXT CHAPTER

In chapter seven, learn about the Old Age Security (OAS) benefits and determine how much to expect. Will you be impacted by the clawback?

- 7 -

OLD AGE SECURITY

Aunt Diggy handed Bev and Bill a booklet. "The other income security program offered by Human Resources Development Canada (HRDC) is the Old Age Security or OAS as it is commonly called. Do you want to guess how much it will provide?"

Bill quipped, "Not enough to retire at age fifty-five, I'm sure of that. Do I still have to take Bev out for dinner?"

"Most planning involves projections and assumptions but I can say with absolute certainty that you better take Bev out for dinner or you will be in the doghouse."

Bev laughed, "You tell him Aunt Diggy."
Bill just smiled knowing she was right.

Diggy explained, "The OAS system is designed to provide an income at age sixty-five but has some very important distinctions from the Canada Pension Plan.

"First, it is not based on contributions as it is funded out of general tax revenues. Hence, all eligible residents are entitled to it. If you lived in Canada for at least forty years since age eighteen you get the full amount.

"If you have less than forty years then the amount is prorated. For example, if you lived in Canada for only twenty years then the amount would be 20/40 or 50%. In order to qualify you must have been a resident of Canada for at least ten years.

"Second, you can only receive benefits at age sixty-five and do not have the option of a reduced pension at age sixty like CPP. This is very important if you are planning on retiring before age sixty-five and need the Old Age Security cheques each month."

"Figures, just when I thought age sixty might be an option the government goes and makes the rules for each source completely different," pouted Bill.

"Third, if your *individual* net income is high you will be required to pay back your benefits and could lose them altogether.

"Currently in 2003, if your net income is above $57,879, you must repay 15% of all dollars above this amount until your income reaches about $94,148 when you lose all your OAS. This is called a Social Benefit Repayment and is shown on line 235 of your income tax return, but everyone affectionately refers to it as the *clawback*."

"I don't need to see any charts on this," said Bill. "I know there is no money between ages fifty-five and sixty-five so the income column will have a bunch of zeroes in it."

"I had no idea," said Bev. "I see the commercials on TV and hear about people retiring in their fifties all the time."

Diggy said, "I can assure you they are not living off CPP and OAS at age fifty-five. Unless you are wealthy or have a great pension plan you will not maintain the same lifestyle at age fifty-five if you retire.

"The good news is that the average person receives 97% of the maximum OAS so you can reasonably expect about $5,400 a year in today's dollars. It is payable for life and fully indexed for inflation.

"You must apply for OAS and it takes about six months to process your application."

"Why do they need six months? They have known for sixty-five years that I would be collecting and surely they have computers," said Bill expressing his frustration with the system.

"My advice is to follow their guidelines or you may encounter delays. They have millions of retired Canadians and like a lot of government offices they don't have the resources they would like, so don't take it out on those nice people who are doing their best with what they have. In fact, I have a friend who works at the HRDC office and she wonders why everyone waits until the day before they need the cheque when they have also known for sixty-five years that they are retiring," said Aunt Diggy with a smile.

"I'd like to show you a very interesting chart showing the OAS Income Replacement amounts. Since it is a flat amount, those with lower incomes will receive a higher percentage of replacement income than those that earn higher incomes. In this case Bev, you will benefit more than Bill even though you both receive the same amount."

"I don't understand," said Bev. "If we receive the same amount how do I benefit more?"

Diggy explained, "Since your income level is

OAS INCOME REPLACEMENT

Current Income Level	OAS Benefit	Replacement Income
$10,000	$5,440	54%
$20,000	$5,440	27%
$30,000	$5,440	18%
$40,000	$5,440	14%
$60,000	$5,440	9%
$80,000	$2,720*	3%
$100,000	$0*	0%

* Reduced due to Clawback

lower, the percentage of that income that is replaced by OAS is higher than Bill's OAS replacement."

"Clearly, this flat benefit system benefits those individuals at lower income levels. Those at the highest level will receive less due to the clawback. Bill, the OAS will replace about 9% of your $60,000 income and 27% of Bev's $20,000 income.

"The following chart will illustrate your income from OAS alone."

SNAPSHOT OF OAS AT AGE 55

Bill's Age	Income Need	OAS Bill	OAS Bev	Total Income
55	$50,000	$0	$0	$0
56	$51,000	$0	$0	$0
57	$52,020	$0	$0	$0
58	$53,060	$0	$0	$0
59	$54,122	$0	$0	$0
60	$55,204	$0	$0	$0
61	$56,308	$0	$0	$0
62	$57,434	$0	$0	$0
63	$58,583	$0	$0	$0
64	$59,755	$0	$0	$0
65	$60,950	$6,631	$0	$7,139
70	$67,293	$7,322	$7,322	$14,644
75	$74,297	$8,084	$8,084	$16,168
80	$82,030	$8,925	$8,925	$17,850
85	$90,568	$9,854	$9,854	$19,708
90	$99,994	$10,880	$10,880	$21,760

"Clearly there will be no income from OAS between the ages of fifty-five and sixty-five for Bill, and then Bev must wait another five years to collect. If you retire at age fifty-five you must find other sources to provide an income.

"Now do you understand why most Canadians can't retire at age fifty-five or even age sixty unless they have resources other than government plans? How do you feel about your retirement plan now?"

"Well, it doesn't look that great but I still have my pension plan and RRSPs to rely on so I am sure I will be just fine," Bill said cautiously knowing that he might be in for some more unexpected surprises. "I can't wait to see the surprises that are in store for me," he said, tongue in cheek. "Every time you ask me a question Aunt Diggy the answer means less money. I value your time but I am just a little frustrated with myself for not taking the time to look into my finances earlier."

"Bill and I should have done this years ago. I am certainly not feeling any pressure so why wouldn't everyone do this? I have a younger brother and sister-in-law who definitely need to see you. I'll pass along your card and have them call you if that is okay."

"I would be glad to help out," replied Aunt

Diggy."

"You must find this career very rewarding," said Bill as he took a bite of cheese bread.

"Yes, I love to help people and I am fascinated by financial planning so I get to do both."

"It is obvious that you are very passionate about this," said Bev.

"Although this probably will not impact you, it is important to go over the OAS clawback so you understand how it works and can plan to avoid it."

OAS CLAWBACK

"I had no idea that high income earners lost their OAS or part of it," Bev said surprised.

"Yes, those rumours that the rich do not pay tax are not always accurate although they have access to accountants and planners to help take advantage of strategies.

"The clawback will impact you only after your individual net income rises above $57,879 (2003). For each dollar earned of net income above $58,000 or so, you will have to repay 15% until you reach about $94,000 of net income when you lose the entire benefit. The following chart will help put this into perspective."

OLD AGE SECURITY (OAS) 2003
Effective January 1, 2003 - March 31, 2003

Individual Net Income	Annual Clawback	Maximum Annual Benefit	Maximum Monthly Benefit
< $57,879	$0	$5,440	$453
$60,000	$318	$5,122	$427
$65,000	$1,068	$4,372	$364
$70,000	$1,818	$3,622	$302
$75,000	$2,568	$2,872	$239
$80,000	$3,318	$2,122	$177
$85,000	$4,068	$1,372	$114
$90,000	$4,818	$622	$52
> $94,148	$5,440	$0	$0

* See page 174 for 2004 Rates

"An eligible individual with a net income of less than $57,879 will get the full $5,440 a year and the person with a net income greater than $94,148 will receive nothing.

"Since your projected retirement income is lower than the individual threshold for the clawback you should receive the full benefit. Let's put this all together in the chart showing your income snapshot at age fifty-five with just the income sources from the government including CPP and OAS."

INCOME AT AGE 55
(CPP + OAS)

Bill's Age	Income Need	Total Income	% of Need	Shortfall / Surplus
55	$50,000	$0	0%	($50,000)
56	$51,000	$0	0%	($51,000)
57	$52,020	$0	0%	($52,020)
58	$53,060	$0	0%	($53,060)
59	$54,122	$0	0%	($54,122)
60	$55,204	$7,431	13%	($47,773)
61	$56,308	$7,580	13%	($48,728)
62	$57,434	$7,731	13%	($49,703)
63	$58,583	$7,886	13%	($50,697)
64	$59,755	$8,044	13%	($51,711)
65	$60,950	$19,445	32%	($41,505)
70	$67,293	$28,231	42%	($39,062)
75	$74,297	$31,169	42%	($43,128)
80	$82,030	$34,413	42%	($47,617)
85	$90,568	$37,995	42%	($52,573)
90	$99,994	$41,950	42%	($58,044)

"What conclusions can you draw from this?" asked Aunt Diggy directly to Bill.

"There goes the sailboat and me retiring at age fifty-five," replied Bill sounding frustrated.

Bev said, "You knew this was unrealistic going in."

"Truthfully, I didn't know it was this bad but I guess a little dose of reality is good. Better to find out now than later. Speaking of later, will I have enough at sixty-five?"

Diggy suggested, "Let's finish the plan at age fifty-five and look at the numbers and then determine if we need to look at age sixty-five. I can tell you that retirement at age fifty-five is unrealistic in most cases but it is a completely different situation at age sixty-five.

"However, you should make sure you are covered in the event you lose your job or are unable to work before your retirement kicks in. Remind me to talk to you about disability, life, and critical illness insurance to ensure you are covered.

"So you can't retire off the government at age fifty-five which is probably a good thing if you look at it from a taxpayer's perspective. Let's review your other sources of income like RRSPs and pension plans through work."

"I can hardly wait," said Bill sarcastically. Bev gave him a nudge to smarten up.

SUMMARY OF LEARNING

- OAS benefits begin as early as age sixty-five. You do not have the option of taking a reduced benefit early like CPP.

- The benefit is based on residency. The annual maximum benefit is $5,440 and the average individual receives 97% of the maximum.

- Individuals with incomes above $57,879 will lose fifteen percent of their benefits above this income level until net income reaches $94,148 where they lose it all.

- OAS is payable for life and fully indexed for inflation each quarter the payments are adjusted.

NEXT CHAPTER

In chapter eight, confirm your understanding of RRSP basics and determine the income level you can expect from your accumulated savings.

- 8 -

RRSPs

"I see you already have RRSPs but let's review the basics to make sure we have the same understanding. There are several features to RRSPs including:

"**First**, contributions are tax deductible. You can deduct the amount of your contribution (within limits) thereby reducing your taxable income. Since you are taxed on the amount of money you expect to make, most individuals who contribute to an RRSP will get an income tax refund as they have paid tax on the higher level of income, or the amount owing will be reduced (see Chapter 5 on Taxation).

"**Second**, the income grows tax-free within the plan and is only taxable upon withdrawal. This is significant because the sheltered income grows at a much higher rate than unsheltered income. In other words, rather than pay the taxes each year, you can invest those funds and benefit from the earnings.

"**Third**, there are limits on how much you can contribute since it is based on your earned income and other retirement plans you may have through work.

"**Fourth**, if you don't use your RRSP

contribution room, you can carry it forward and use it in the future."

"Yes, I am clear on the basics of RRSPs," said Bev.

"Okay. Bill, I see from your statements that you have accumulated approximately $100,000 in RRSPs."

"Yes, I'm very proud of that because $100,000 is a lot of money and I've been saving for years. It was actually worth almost $125,000 but the markets have been bad the last three years."

"You have done well Bill, but I have a few questions for you."

"Oh no, not again. Please don't tell me it isn't enough, or the government is going to take it, or that I'll lose my CPP. I'm not sure if I want to hear the questions," said Bill jokingly as he really did want to know. He thought he might be penalized for saving on his own and that was the last thing he wanted to hear.

"You're getting good at this Bill, you must know what my first question is going to be."

"Let me guess, how much income do I think it will provide at age fifty-five?"

"Bingo!" shouted Aunt Diggy impressed with Bill. "How much income do you expect?"

"I really don't know," said Bill.

"There are three factors to consider. First, how long you need the money to last, second, what rate of return you can expect, and third, how much money you want to leave behind for your estate."

"I'll need the money for life. Let's assume there is nothing for the kids. Anything I have when I die will go to Bev and the kids but let's just assume I will need it all for now."

"As we said earlier, the average lifespan for men is about eighty years and for women it is about eighty-two. I suggest that the plan assume the money must last until Bill is age ninety and Bev is age eighty-five. This will allow a three-year cushion in case you live a few years longer than the average person."

"What happens if I live longer than ninety?" said Bill thinking that he might just live to one hundred and didn't want to run out of money.

"You still have CPP, OAS, company pension etc. which are payable for life so don't let that worry you right now. Again, we will do an annual review of your financial situation and adjust as circumstances change. We can always take more money at any time but this will be at the expense of less money down the road.

"The second component is the rate of return

that is dependant on where you invest. If you like guaranteed products like GICs I generally use a 5% return for projections but if you have it all in equity-based funds I would use 9%. However, you will not get a perfect 9% return every year. The markets fluctuate so one year you might get 12% and another year only 2%. I find these numbers are a reasonable projection but keep in mind we want to be conservative. If I think the markets will do 10% and your projection says 9% then you will be ahead of plan. Whereas, if I project at 12% and the markets do 10% then you are behind your plan. It is all about setting realistic expectations.

"The following chart will show what return to expect as part of your plan. I see you completed the risk tolerance questions with Jenn and you are a middle of the road investor who wants some growth in equities but doesn't like too much risk. This translates into a profile #3 which translates into a portfolio consisting of about 50% in equity funds and about 50% in either GICs or Bond funds. This is a nicely balanced approach to investing and is similar to how major pension plans are managed where they put about 55% to 60% in equities and about 40% to 45% in bonds. The following chart will put the different portfolio mixes and their corresponding estimated returns into perspective."

Profile	Equities @ 9%	Fixed Income @ 5%	Expected Rate Blended
1	100%	0%	9%
2	75%	25%	8%
3	50%	50%	7%
4	25%	75%	6%
5	0%	100%	5%

"Assuming you are clear on how we arrived at these estimated rates of return and you are comfortable using the 7% figure, the following chart shows the average returns of funds after the management fees and expenses have been eliminated. Notice how the one-year returns can be quite volatile. In contrast, the ten-year returns are all positive and are in line with our 7% estimated return for your retirement plan."

Fund Category	1 YR	3 YR	5 YR	10 YR
Inflation (CPI)	4.3	2.7	2.4	1.8
1-year GICs	1.6	3.0	3.3	4.0
5-year GICs	4.0	4.5	4.6	5.5
Canadian Equity	(13.5)	(2.2)	2.0	8.8
Canadian Bond	6.5	6.9	4.9	7.1
Canadian Balanced	(6.0)	0.0	2.5	7.5
U.S. Equity (Can. $)	(24.8)	(15.1)	(2.3)	7.1
Global Equity (Can. $)	(20.7)	(14.0)	(1.4)	6.6

As at August 31, 2003

Aunt Diggy further explained, "The average return for Canadian equities over the past fifty years is ten percent if you look at rolling ten-year returns. A six percent return is the average for bond funds over the same period."

"What is a rolling period?" Bev asked.

"A rolling period is when you calculate returns over any ten-year period and roll the dates. For example, the period from 1974-1984 and then 1975-1985 and so on," explained Aunt Diggy.

"Yes, I have seen articles in the paper explaining a rate but it has never been clearly explained like this before. I like the fact that I can see the numbers as they relate to my risk," commented Bill.

"I'm completely in agreement," said Bev.

"The third factor is how long you need the money and how much you would like to have at the end. For example, do you just want to live off the interest or growth or will you slowly use up the principal which will provide a higher annual amount but you will eventually run out?"

"Let's look at taking an even amount each year based on that 7% so that it will run out at age ninety. I might not spend it all but at least I know approximately how much to expect each year." Bill suddenly sounded like he was a retirement planner himself.

"Here is another chart that I put together for this purpose," said Aunt Diggy, handing both Bev and Bill a copy of the chart. "You look at the column that shows your expected rate of return. In this case it is 7%. Follow that column to the number of years, which is thirty-five, and you will see the amount of $7,218 a year. If your $100,000 earned an even 7% annually and you took out $7,218 per year, your money will run out in your ninetieth year."

AUNT DIGGY'S RRSP INCOME ESTIMATOR
($100,000 lump sum)

Years	5%	6%	7%	8%	9%
5	$21,998	$22,396	$22,794	$23,190	$23,586
10	$12,334	$12,818	$13,306	$13,799	$14,295
15	$9,175	$9,713	$10,261	$10,818	$11,382
20	$7,642	$8,225	$8,882	$9,431	$10,050
25	$6,757	$7,380	$8,020	$8,674	$9,340
30	$6,195	$6,854	$7,531	$8,225	$8,930
35	$5,816	$6,507	$7,218	$7,945	$8,682
40	$5,550	$6,270	$7,010	$7,765	$8,528

Step 1:	Find the rate of return e.g. 7%.
Step 2:	Find the number of years capital is required e.g. 35 years
Step 3:	Find the box where they intersect. This number represents the annual payment for that time period (no indexing) based on a $100,000 investment.

"Let's put all the income sources together at age fifty-five."

INCOME AT AGE 55
(CPP, OAS, RRSP)

Bill's Age	Income Need	Total Income	% of Need	Shortfall / Surplus
55	$50,000	$7,218	14%	($42,782)
56	$51,000	$7,218	14%	($43,782)
57	$52,020	$7,218	14%	($44,802)
58	$53,060	$7,218	13%	($45,842)
59	$54,122	$7,218	13%	($46,904)
60	$55,204	$14,649	27%	($40,555)
61	$56,308	$14,798	26%	($41,510)
62	$57,434	$14,949	26%	($42,485)
63	$58,583	$15,104	26%	($43,479)
64	$59,755	$15,262	26%	($44,493)
65	$60,950	$26,663	44%	($34,287)
70	$67,293	$35,449	53%	($31,844)
75	$74,297	$38,387	52%	($35,910)
80	$82,030	$41,631	51%	($40,399)
85	$90,568	$45,213	50%	($45,355)
90	$99,994	$49,168	49%	($50,826)

"What do you think Bill?" asked Aunt Diggy.

"It is starting to look a little better between ages fifty-five and sixty-five but my income is low at age fifty-five. I'm hoping for good things from my company pension plan."

"It is quite clear that you will have substantially less than you need before age sixty-five from your current income sources. You could take more out of your RRSPs in the early years to make up the shortfall but that would be unrealistic because your RRSPs would be depleted early creating a bigger problem down the road."

Bill started to tell Aunt Diggy about his pension plans at work when she said, "What makes you think we are finished talking about your RRSP?"

"I thought this was a little too easy. Okay, what other questions do you have?" said Bill.

"The first issue is to ask if the funds are locked-in, which brings us to the topic of Locked-In Retirement Accounts or LIRAs as they are called in the industry."

Bev said, "There certainly are a lot of acronyms out there. Let's see we covered CPP, OAS, RRSP and now we can add LIRA."

SUMMARY OF LEARNING

- RRSP contribution limits are based on 18% of your earnings from the previous year up to an annual maximum of $14,500. Contributions are tax deductible.

- Tax sheltered contributions grow tax-free within the plan but are taxable upon withdrawal at your marginal tax rate.

- $100,000 will provide an annual taxable income of approximately $7,218 to a fifty-five-year-old until age ninety.

- An individual can carry forward unused contribution room from one year to the next. Effectively, they can contribute and deduct more than $14,500 in a given year.

NEXT CHAPTER

In chapter nine, learn how LIRAs are different from RRSPs and the restrictions that are placed on these plan types.

- 9 -

LOCKED-IN RETIREMENT ACCOUNTS

Bill held up a copy of his statement and said, "I have some money that is *locked-in* guaranteed investment certificates for five years until they mature but I don't know the exact amount. Is that important?"

Aunt Diggy explained, "There are two types of locked-in money and the distinction is important. The first is the type that you just mentioned which is a locked-in *investment*. The second type is a locked-in retirement *account*."

"What is the difference?" questioned Bev.

"The first type, the locked-in *investment* means you generally can't get at that money or that you will have penalties to break that certificate in the case of a GIC. This is not what we mean when we say locked-in retirement account.

"A LIRA refers to money that originated from a pension plan. You can't contribute to a LIRA but you can transfer your pension. This transfer option is normally restricted to members who have terminated employment and left the plan. It is intended to provide a stream of income for life. Unlike RRSPs where you can take the entire amount out if you wish, a LIRA can't be touched in Ontario until you are at least fifty-five years old. However, you can apply for an exception to get at these funds in certain hardship cases. The information is contained on the FSCO website, www.fsco.on.ca. A LIRA is converted to a Locked-in Retirement Income Fund (LRIF) or a Life Income Fund (LIF) once the money is required for retirement. Since the money is intended to be a pension, the pension legislation dictates the minimum and maximum amounts you may take out each year based upon your age."

"I see," said Bill. "And what are the minimum and maximum amounts?"

"For example, with RRSPs, you can take out as much as you want - subject to tax. Once you do take it out you are subject to *minimum* withdrawal rules via a Registered Retirement Income Fund (RRIF). If you look at this chart that amount is 5% in your seventieth year, and varies for future years.

"Locked-in money is subject to the same minimums but you also have *maximum* withdrawal restrictions. At age seventy, the most you can withdraw is a little over 8%. So, although you have some flexibility you are subject to these rules with a LIRA and LIF. With RRSPs, you can withdraw everything and buy a yacht if you want. In contrast, a LIRA will not permit a 100% withdrawal. You have the option of basing the withdrawals on your spouse's age if younger. Depending on the balance each year, the maximum withdrawal could actually be lower from one year to the next."

Bev asked, "Why would the amount be lower in a subsequent year when the maximum withdrawal percentage is higher?"

Aunt Diggy explained, "The withdrawal is based on the account balance at the end of the previous calendar year. If an individual had a balance of $100,000 with a maximum withdrawal of 8% they could withdraw $8,000. However, if the balance declined to $80,000 due to market conditions, they would only have $7,200 if we assume they are allowed a maximum withdrawal of 9%. This understanding is very important to those who require the maximum each year and therefore should not put their account at risk with volatile investments."

LIFE INCOME FUND (LIF) - WITHDRAWALS

Age	Minimum %	Maximum %	Minimum $100,000	Maximum $100,000
55	2.86%	6.51%	$2,860	$6,510
56	2.94%	6.57%	$2,940	$6,570
57	3.03%	6.63%	$3,030	$6,630
58	3.13%	6.70%	$3,130	$6,700
59	3.23%	6.77%	$3,230	$6,770
60	3.33%	6.85%	$3,330	$6,850
61	3.45%	6.94%	$3,450	$6,940
62	3.57%	7.04%	$3,570	$7,040
63	3.70%	7.14%	$3,700	$7,140
64	3.84%	7.26%	$3,840	$7,260
65	4.00%	7.38%	$4,000	$7,380
66	4.17%	7.52%	$4,170	$7,520
67	4.35%	7.67%	$4,350	$7,670
68	4.55%	7.83%	$4,550	$7,830
69	4.76%	8.02%	$4,760	$8,020
70	5.00%	8.22%	$5,000	$8,220
71	7.38%	8.45%	$7,380	$8,450
72	7.48%	8.71%	$7,480	$8,710
73	7.59%	9.00%	$7,590	$9,000
74	7.71%	9.34%	$7,710	$9,340
75	7.85%	9.71%	$7,850	$9,710
76	7.99%	10.15%	$7,990	$10,150
77	8.15%	10.66%	$8,150	$10,660
78	8.33%	11.25%	$8,330	$11,250
79	8.53%	11.96%	$8,530	$11,960

*Annuity must be purchased at age 80

SUMMARY OF LEARNING

- The funds within a LIRA originate from a pension plan and are intended to provide a lifetime stream of income.

- Withdrawals from a LIRA are not permitted until age fifty-five. An individual can apply to the Financial Services Commission of Ontario to release funds due to a hardship condition. Their website is www.fsco.on.ca and the application forms and list of hardship conditions can be found on their site.

- Withdrawals from a locked-in account are subject to both *minimum* and *maximum* withdrawal limits.

NEXT CHAPTER

In chapter ten, learn about Spousal RRSPs. How do they work and who can benefit from them?

- 10 -

SPOUSAL RRSPs

"Have you heard of Spousal RRSPs?" asked Aunt Diggy.

Bev replied, "I've heard the name but we don't know what they are."

"To understand Spousal RRSPs it is important that we remember the basics of taxation that we discussed previously. The main issue is that couples with the same household income may pay different amounts of tax. The difference is due to a tax system that taxes family members as individuals and not as families. Hence, some families pay more tax on the same household income as other families. This isn't treating couples equally.

"The tax system isn't perfect so it is important to understand the rules. To correct this situation Canada Customs and Revenue Agency (CCRA) established Spousal RRSPs as a form of income splitting."

"I've heard of Spousal RRSPs but I've never actually done anything or at least I don't think I have," said Bill.

"I have reviewed your statement Bill and you have not designated any of your contributions as spousal. In fact, Bill is the contributor and annuitant for all your RRSPs."

"How do Spousal RRSPs work?" asked Bev with keen interest thinking that maybe they could save some tax dollars here.

"One spouse can contribute to the other spouse's RRSP. The contributing spouse gets the tax deduction based on their tax rate and it counts against the contributor's RRSP contribution room. When it comes time to take out the money it is taxed in the receiving spouse's hands at a lower rate. There is one small rule called the Spousal Attribution Rule that states, if you made a Spousal RRSP contribution in the current or previous two years, that is CCRA lingo for three years, the contributor pays the tax."

"Why would they have such a rule if it just confuses people?" asked Bill.

"Spousal RRSPs are designed for long term planning to correct the inequalities in the system. They are not designed for somebody who wants to put the money in today and get 46% back and take it out tomorrow and pay 22%."

Bill was still unclear on how this would benefit the situation. "Could you provide an example please to show the math?"

Tax savings with a Spousal RRSP

"Bill, in your situation you make $60,000 so your marginal tax rate is about 33%. Bev makes $20,000 and her marginal tax rate is 22%. (Refer to chapter five on taxation.) You both have RRSP contribution room so let's assume as a family you have $1,000 in available funds to contribute to an RRSP.

"Bill, if you contribute the $1,000, you will save $330 in taxes ($1,000 @ 33%). Bev, if you contribute the $1,000, you will save $220 in taxes ($1,000 @ 22%).

"Now, who should make the contribution?"

Bill said, "That's easy, I would rather get a $330 refund than $220 refund as that extra 50% is much better in my pocket than the government's coffer."

"Let's expand assuming tax rates will not change in the future and your income levels will be approximately the same in relation to each other. How much tax will you pay Bill when the funds are withdrawn?"

"About 33%."

"What rate of tax will you pay Bev?"

"About 22%."

"Okay, now I'm really confused. What is the point of getting a bigger refund if you have to pay more back in the end?" asked Bill.

"Bill, what if you could get the 33% savings now instead of Bev's 22% and then pay 22% when you took it out instead of 33%. Would that interest you?"

"It sure would. But I'm not going to do anything illegal, am I? That sounds a little too good to be true."

"A Spousal RRSP would designate Bill as the contributor so he receives a 33% tax savings at the time of the contribution and then Bev takes it out down the road and pays 22% tax at retirement."

Bev said, "You have got to be kidding, that is fantastic, I had heard of Spousal RRSPs but that is a great strategy; and they allow you to do this?"

"That sounds great to me," said Bill. "Sign me up. I want to save money on tax."

"It isn't that easy."

"Oh no, not again. Please don't tell me I can't use a Spousal RRSP. I can't take much more of this," said Bill half joking.

"The designation must be made at the time of the contribution and you can't change it after the fact. If you made personal contributions you can't switch them down the road."

"That really makes me mad. Why does the government put in these rules to help people and then put all these restrictions? Why should we be penalized for not knowing the rules? We elect these folks and they are supposed to help us. The average working Canadian doesn't understand these things."

"I could not agree with you more Bill and it would be nice if they allowed this. Perhaps you can write a letter to your elected official. That is the reason why I tell all my extended family about Spousal RRSPs and always look for an opportunity to save taxes. We should be thankful they have Spousal RRSPs and whomever you were dealing with before missed a real opportunity here to help. We cannot change the past but we can certainly look out for these things going forward."

"I know a few people who might want to use Spousal RRSPs," said Bev. "Are they for anyone who has a spouse?"

"That is a great question. Usually we try to get the biggest tax deduction when making a contribution so the higher income level should claim it and pay the lowest level upon taking it.

"The traditional family from our generation should use Spousal RRSPs but many families today are seeing equal incomes or in many cases the wife makes a lot more than the husband."

"It's about time women got paid fairly," said Bev giving Bill a gentle elbow to his side and a look that he wasn't about to challenge."

"If there are different tax brackets now or if they are expected to be different in the future then you should consider Spousal RRSPs. A certified financial planner or an accountant can help make this determination in your individual circumstance. In some cases, one spouse clearly makes more today but the projection could look completely different in the future. This aspect of your retirement plan should be reviewed each year before making your regular RRSP contributions. Remember, you should work with a certified financial planner and follow your plan."

SUMMARY OF LEARNING

- The spouse in a higher tax bracket contributes to their spouse's RRSP. The higher income spouse receives the tax deduction.

- The annuitant spouse is taxed upon the withdrawal.

- The Spousal Attribution Rule is three years.

- Designation must be made at the time of the contribution.

- Spousal RRSPs level the taxation playing field for couples.

NEXT CHAPTER

In chapter eleven, learn about the different types of pension plans to determine which type you have. There are several questions that you must ask and they differ depending on the type of plan you have.

- 11 -

PENSION PLANS

"Bill, thanks for bringing in your pension booklet from work and a copy of your most recent statement. The first step is to determine what type of pension plan you belong to.

"The two main classifications are Defined Benefit (DB) versus Defined Contribution (DC) and there is a huge difference between them.

"The first type is called a Defined Benefit plan because the benefit is defined by a formula which may be used to calculate your pension benefit. These are the traditional forms of pension with over five million Canadians in these plans versus about 800,000 in DC plans. The number of DB plans has remained constant over the period from 1995-2000 whereas DC plans grew 38% over the same period of time.

"We will review the basics of Defined Benefit plans first. The benefit is defined as a set percentage of your income per each year of service times the number of years of service. For example, a 2% benefit plan could provide 70% of your income in retirement for an employee who has thirty-five years of service (35 x 2%). For example, if your income was $50,000 per year, you would receive an annual benefit of $35,000 for life (2% x 35 years = 70% of $50,000).

"The eligibility for full retirement benefits is based on a magic number, which is a combination of age and years of service and typically this would be ninety. If you are sixty years old with thirty years of service you will be entitled to full benefits. You can usually retire earlier but the pension will be reduced just like CPP since you will be collecting for a longer period of time.

"The Defined Benefit plans are intended and designed for the traditional employee who works for a company for many years until normal retirement age.

"The employee, called a member, doesn't make any investment decision as the responsibility to provide the benefit resides with the employer."

"Okay, I understand the Defined Benefit plans; now how do the Defined Contribution plans work?" asked Bill.

"The Defined Contribution plans are completely different because the *contribution* is defined by a formula but the benefit is completely undefined.

"Typically, the employer will allow the member to contribute a maximum percentage of their income and the employer will match it. For example, if you make $50,000 a year in a 5% plan, you will be eligible to contribute $2,500 ($50,000 x 5%) and the employer will match your contributions by putting in $2,500.

"The member makes the investment decision and whatever is in the pot at retirement is the amount that is used to purchase a stream of income at retirement. For example, if there is $500,000 in the pot and you earn an 8% return, the benefit would generate $40,000 a year without touching the principal. However, if rates decreased from 8% to 4% you get only $20,000 so the benefit is completely left up to how your investment makes out. Bill, do you know what type you have?"

"Actually, I have both types," said Bill wondering if that made any sense.

"Some companies do indeed have both types of plans. Bev, do you have a pension plan or group retirement savings plan at work?"

"No, I don't have any plans. They pay a great hourly rate but the benefits are not very good."

"Do you understand the basic difference between the two plan types?"

"Yes," Bill replied.

SUMMARY OF LEARNING

- Under a Defined Benefit (DB) pension plan, the benefit is defined by a formula. In contrast, a Defined Contribution (DC) plan defines the contribution limits and the benefit is unknown.

- The employer is responsible for making the investment decisions under the DB plan whereas the employee takes on this responsibility under a DC plan.

- There are more of the traditional DB plans in place but there is a shift to DC plans as they are better suited for the modern employee who will have more than one employer during their lifetime.

NEXT CHAPTER

In chapter twelve, learn the six critical things you need to know about your Defined Benefit pension plan. See what surprises are in store for Bill when Aunt Diggy reviews his DB pension plan.

- 12 -

DEFINED BENEFIT PENSION PLANS

"A quick review of your pension booklet tells me you have a Defined Benefit plan Bill. Right here is a section called "Benefit" and you can see that it states:

Benefit is defined as 1% of the average income of your last three years for each year of service to a maximum of thirty-five years. Benefits will be reduced for those members whose combination of years of service plus age does not equal or exceed ninety. The minimum age to retire is fifty-five and normal retirement age is sixty-five.

"There is a lot of information in that statement but let's refer to your benefit statement to try to make sense of it all.

"Let's start with your income level for calculating your benefit. Right here it shows the average of your last three years as $60,000 so the benefit will be based on that number if you retired today.

"The next section shows that you have twenty-five years of eligible pension service with the company at age fifty-five."

"Right, I've been there twenty-seven years but I

didn't join the pension for the first two years so my service for pension is twenty-five years."

"The benefit is 1% for each year of service so putting it all together we have: ($60,000 x 1% x 25 years) which equals $15,000 per year for life."

"That was pretty simple. I get $15,000 a year for life. At least this type of plan is looked after and I don't need to worry about taking this at age fifty-five," said Bill. "That is unless you have something to tell me," he said half joking.

"Bill, these plans can be very complicated and each one is unique. There are some very important things I need to point out that can significantly impact your retirement income."

"Oh no, not again. I already know that retirement at age fifty-five is not realistic but please don't tell me I am not going to get $15,000 or that I cannot take my pension at fifty-five."

Bev turned to Bill and said, "Have you ever read your pension statement that they send you every single year? Do you ever look at your booklet? Did you attend any of those information sessions at work?"

Bill just turned to Bev and said, "I have not been paying much attention to retirement planning but at least I am here now and ready to listen."

"I will break the questions down for you one by

one as each one has significant implications and you need to obtain the answers to these questions. Some may be applicable while others will not."

#1. Is your pension plan indexed?

"Indexing is a term which means your plan benefit amount is adjusted for the cost of living and therefore will generally increase with the cost of living but will not decrease if the cost of living goes down. Hence, if the cost of living goes up 3%, your pension benefit will go up 3% the following year."

"I thought it was standard that everyone got a cost of living increase. Are you trying to tell me that they don't increase the payments when the cost of living goes up each year?" said Bill.

Bev thought to herself that this was very important and all employees should know whether it is indexed or not.

"Indexing is not a requirement and certainly it costs the employer less if it isn't. I read an article recently that stated about 50% of the plans are indexed but of the 50% most have restrictions in that they only partially index the payment or they have a maximum level. For example, the CPP used to be designed to increase only if rates were above 3%.

Imagine what happens if you have five years of 2% inflation. Your costs have gone up by more than 10% and you have received no increase. The CPP has changed and now offers full indexing.

Some plans have a maximum so if inflation were 12% you would only get 8% for example. Our earlier discussion showed how these increases can be substantial over time.

"Fortunately, your plan is fully indexed for inflation. The wording on your contract states:

Benefit payments are fully indexed each year in line with increases in the Consumer Price Index."

"Well for once there is good news but I should have known this. It is my own fault for not reading the booklets. I still feel the employer has a responsibility to ensure us average working guys understand the plan."

#2. Is your benefit reduced if taken early?

"The booklet states that you must be at least age fifty-five to retire. To receive a full, unreduced pension, you must have a combination of years of service and age that total ninety. Each year of retirement prior to obtaining this ninety factor will result in a reduction of 6% for each year.

"Bill, in your situation at age fifty-five with twenty-five years of service your number is eighty (55+25). For each year you work this number will increase by two since you are also one year older. In five years' time you will have fulfilled the requirements for a full pension. However, if you retire at age fifty-five with a magic number of eighty, your pension benefits will be reduced by 6% a year for each of the five years you have taken it early. The $15,000 you were expecting has just been reduced to $10,500."

"I would say that that is an important thing to know," said Bev. "I wonder how many folks at the plant don't even have a clue about that."

Bill looked pale. Although he didn't plan on retiring at age fifty-five, he thought he would receive $15,000. "I can't understand why they do not make these plans clearer. I am going to make sure the other guys like Brad and Duane know about this."

"The following chart will show your Defined Benefit entitlement from the company at age fifty-five."

Pension Bill	Pension Bev	Total Income	Bill's Age	Income Need
$10,500	$0	$10,500	55	$50,000
$10,710	$0	$10,710	56	$51,000
$10,924	$0	$10,924	57	$52,020
$11,143	$0	$11,143	58	$53,060
$11,366	$0	$11,366	59	$54,122
$11,593	$0	$11,593	60	$55,204
$11,825	$0	$11,825	61	$56,308
$12,061	$0	$12,061	62	$57,434
$12,302	$0	$12,302	63	$58,583
$12,548	$0	$12,548	64	$59,755
$12,799	$0	$12,799	65	$60,950
$14,132	$0	$14,132	70	$67,293
$15,602	$0	$15,602	75	$74,297
$17,226	$0	$17,226	80	$82,030
$19,019	$0	$19,019	85	$90,568
$20,999	$0	$20,999	90	$99,994

"It is an indexed amount and starts from day one. See how the amount doubles over time from $10,500 to $20,999. The following income projection should put this into perspective."

INCOME AT AGE 55
(CPP, OAS, RRSP, DB Pension)

Bill's Age	Income Need	Total Income	% of Need	Shortfall / Surplus
55	$50,000	$17,718	35%	($32,282)
56	$51,000	$17,928	35%	($33,072)
57	$52,020	$18,142	35%	($33,878)
58	$53,060	$18,361	35%	($34,699)
59	$54,122	$18,584	34%	($35,538)
60	$55,204	$26,242	48%	($28,962)
61	$56,308	$26,643	47%	($29,685)
62	$57,434	$27,010	47%	($30,424)
63	$58,583	$27,406	47%	($31,177)
64	$59,755	$27,810	47%	($31,945)
65	$60,950	$39,462	65%	($21,488)
70	$67,293	$49,581	74%	($17,712)
75	$74,297	$53,989	73%	($20,308)
80	$82,030	$58,857	72%	($23,173)
85	$90,568	$64,232	71%	($26,336)
90	$99,994	$70,167	70%	($29,827)

"Well, I am doing a little better but it is becoming very clear that retirement at age fifty-five, like the guy on television, is not going to happen. I am looking forward to seeing how the age sixty-five snapshot looks because I am starting to think we might have to sell the family home and I don't want to do that."

#3. *Does your plan have a bridge payment?*

"Your pension does NOT have a bridge payment Bill."

"What is a bridge payment?" asked Bill thinking this was a silly name.

"A bridge payment is applicable to certain DB plans whereby the plan recognizes that you could be eligible for full pension before age sixty-five. Since CPP doesn't provide the normal pension until age sixty-five, the company pension will provide a payment to replace CPP from ages fifty-five to sixty-five.

"If you had a bridge, you would receive a payment equivalent to CPP if it were to start at age fifty-five and then stop at age sixty-five when it would be replaced with CPP."

"Interesting," said Bill. "I have never heard of such a thing but it is a good idea. I now understand why they call it a bridge as it bridges you to full retirement benefits. I wonder why we do not have one?"

"There is a cost to this benefit and sometimes it is optional to pay for it. Usually you get the bridge at the expense of lower overall pension but many plan sponsors would argue that this is a bonus that is provided. If the members of the plan do not make an issue out of a bridge then the plan will not provide it.

"For anyone who is retiring before age sixty-five it is very important to find out if their plan has a bridge payment and, if it is optional, to determine if the extra cost is worth it. Most Canadians are short in the income department when they retire at age fifty-five so this would definitely make a difference.

"Generally speaking, if you expect to get $10,000 a year from CPP then your bridge will be $10,000 until age sixty-five and then it will go to zero with the assumption that CPP will provide approximately the same amount."

"I know my plan does not have it now but I am going to raise this with the company pension representative to find out if she can put a price to this. We should be negotiating these things into the contract and into the pension plan."

#4: *Is your pension integrated with CPP?*

"One very important question to answer is: Is your plan integrated?"

"I do not understand why pensions must use complicated terms that nobody understands. I can just imagine having a conversation at the plant and asking if the plan is integrated," laughed Bill.

"This is one of the reasons many members do not read their booklets, because of the terminology. Integrated simply means that the pension plan is designed to incorporate Canada Pension Plan benefits into the plan to provide a certain overall level of retirement income and is designed for age sixty-five as the normal retirement age."

"Can you give me an example?" said Bev. This didn't make any sense to her either. How could an employer determine what Canada Pension Plan would pay?

"Since an employer knows that CPP will provide a certain amount of retirement income they design the company pension plan to take this into account. For example, if they know CPP will replace 25% of your income and they want you to have 70% then the company pension will provide 45%. However, since CPP only pays 25% of your income up to YMPE (Yearly Maximum Pensionable Earnings) ($40,000) then the plan will have to provide much more for those who earn more than $40,000 a year. It is estimated that CPP provides the equivalent of 0.6% for each year of service so if a plan wants to provide 2% including CPP then the company pension will provide about 1.4% for your income up to YMPE and the full 2% for income above that level.

Income Level	CPP	Company Pension	Total Benefit
<$40,000	0.6%	1.4%	2.0%
>$40,000	0.0%	2.0%	2.0%

"How would you feel if you retired at age fifty-five and were told your company pension benefit was 2% per year which worked out to $25,000 a year including the bridge benefit payment? You receive this amount for ten years and then you apply for CPP and are told you will get $10,000 a year.

"Your expectation is $25,000 plus $10,000 for an income of $35,000 so you go and lease a new Cadillac.

"Your first CPP cheque arrives based on your $10,000 annual benefit and you receive your normal pension cheque and it is based on an annual income of $15,000 versus the normal $25,000 that you have come to expect during the past ten years.

"You call your employer to explain the error only to learn that it is correct. In fact, they quote directly from your pension booklet a statement that reads:

Your plan is integrated with CPP. Once CPP commences your pension will be reduced by the equivalent amount...

"How are you feeling right now Bill?"

"Please tell me that my plan is not integrated with Canada Pension Plan."

"Your plan is not integrated with CPP so you do not need to worry about this. Whatever your company pension provides will be above and beyond any benefits from the government in the form of OAS and CPP.

"Most people spend more time and effort shopping for a car than they do reading their pension statement and planning for their retirement. Obviously there are some very key questions here. The bottom line is that we don't want surprises. What you expect to receive should match what you receive. It isn't very often that somebody is surprised because his or her payment goes up."

"I very much appreciate your pointing all that information out but let's get to the chart showing how much I will get from just my pension and then when it is put together with the other income sources," said Bill."

"There is more that you need to know Bill."

#5. *What happens if the retiree dies?*

"The first is regarding health care benefits. Your plan is excellent in that retired employees receive the same health and dental benefits as working employees but most plans cut you off or reduce the benefits. With drug costs escalating this could really impact your income requirements in retirement."

"Doesn't the government provide benefits for prescriptions?" questioned Bev.

"They do, but with most government programs there are restrictions and I can almost guarantee you that your private plan is much better than the government plan. The government plan is not intended to be top of the line rather it provides very basic services for those in need that can't afford it.

"There is one item to consider that is very important for Bev to understand."

"What does Bill's pension have to do with me?" asked Bev.

"What happens to Bill's pension if he were to die before you? There is legislation to protect spouses who are entitled to continue receiving benefits upon the death of the pensioner. Usually this is 60%. Bill's plan will provide 60% of his monthly benefit to you should you outlive him and be payable for your life."

"That makes me feel very comfortable. I never really thought about it; I guess I just assumed it would be there," said Bev.

"What happens if I outlive Bev? Do the kids get the payments or do they stop?" asked Bill.

"The plan might have a guaranteed period which means you are guaranteed a certain number of benefit payments. Ten years is typical with your beneficiaries receiving a lump sum representing the remainder of the ten years. If you both died in five years the kids would get the remaining five years worth of guaranteed payments. If you both die and there is no guarantee, your payments will stop.

"Bill before you ask, I have already checked your plan and there is no guaranteed period applicable so if you both die the payments will stop. However, your normal lifespan will far exceed the typical ten-year guarantee."

"I know," said Bill, "but I've worked so hard. If we happen to die who gets our money?"

"The money goes back into the plan to pay for those members who live longer than normal. Remember that it is based on the assumption that the average employee will have an average lifespan."

#6. What is the Pension Adjustment?

"CCRA wants everyone to have the same benefit to sheltering income via RRSP and other retirement plans since they have maximum contribution limits. They recognize that since the amount is capped it would not be fair for one person to shelter money in their RRSP plus their pension plan when others only have an RRSP without a pension plan. So they introduced the concept called a Pension Adjustment or PA. What it does is recognizes and tries to calculate the benefit from the pension and they subtract this amount from what you can contribute to your RRSP. For example, if the Pension Adjustment is $5,000 and you can contribute $10,000 to your RRSP, then you will only be able to contribute $5,000. With Defined Benefit plans the Pension Adjustment is calculated by a formula as follows:

(9 x Benefit) - $600

"If the annual benefit is 2% of your income, then 9 x 2% = 18% of your income. Since you can only accumulate RRSP room up to 18% of your income you will only have $600 of RRSP room. In your situation Bill, the adjustment will be $4,800. Since you make $60,000 it will be:

9 x $600 = $5,400 - $600 = $4,800."

"Now, I knew there was an adjustment but I had no idea how it was calculated."

"You are just a wealth of knowledge now," said Bev. "I bet you can't wait to go back to the plant and show everyone how smart you are," she joked.

"Since your contribution room would be 18% of $60,000, you are allowed to have a contribution of $10,800. However, you must subtract the $4,800 so you now can contribute $6,000 plus any unused carry forward room."

"Since I only plan on contributing $5,000 a year I will have lots of extra room," said Bill.

SUMMARY OF LEARNING

- DB plans define the benefit by formula and the benefit can be calculated in advance using income and inflation assumptions.

- A combination of age plus years of service determine your eligibility. Ninety is a common magic number to use with a 6% reduction for each year retired before this.

- About one half the plans are indexed for inflation.

- A bridge payment may provide a benefit similar to CPP between ages fifty-five and sixty-five.

- Certain DB pension plans are integrated with CPP to provide an overall level of retirement income.

NEXT CHAPTER

In chapter thirteen, find out what Bill needs to know about his Defined Contribution pension plan. Will he be pleasantly surprised?

- 13 -

DEFINED CONTRIBUTION PLANS

"These plans are designed for today's workforce who are likely to have multiple employers during their working years. Employers like the DC plans for their simplicity and ability to limit the employer's liability to the current year's contribution. The employee, or member, as they are commonly called, contributes a certain amount each year and the employer will match some or all of that contribution within limits. They are also called Money Purchase Pension Plans (MPPP) because the accumulated money is used to purchase a stream of income as a pension plan. Think of them as self-directed pension plans.

"Upon retirement, the member invests the money and whatever amount is in the account is what they have to provide a lifetime stream of income. This can either be a life annuity or managed with a LIF or LRIF plan subject to the minimum and maximum withdrawal limitations.

"Depending on how the money is invested the member could be better or worse in retirement so it is very important to monitor the performance of these plans. The future income stream is not guaranteed and the employee is responsible for their future."

"Sounds a lot like a Registered Retirement Savings Plan to me," said Bill.

"Yes, they are very similar but remember they are governed by pension legislation and are subject to those minimum and maximum restrictions that we discussed earlier.

"Bill's plan matches his contributions up to YMPE ($39,300 in 2003) at 1% of income. In addition, 2% of income above YMPE is matched. If YMPE is rounded to $40,000 then 1% of $40,000 = $400 plus 2% of ($60,000 - $40,000) = $400 for a total of $800 of contributions that are eligible for matching by the employer. He will see $1,600 going into the plan each year and this amount will increase as his income goes up."

"I like seeing the company's money on the statement and it shows as real dollars," said Bev. "Is there anything else we need to know about DC plans?"

"It is not applicable in your case but the term 'vesting' is very important to understand. If you notice on the statement you have an account called *employee* and another one called *employer*. They keep this separate because you are only entitled to the employer contributions once you are vested.

Normally, vesting is two years. If you left the plan early you would forfeit the contributions made by your employer. Just think how you would feel if you gave up thousands of dollars that you expected because you left three days early."

"Nobody in their right mind would do that," said Bill, "assuming they knew what vesting was."

"With your current balance of about $50,000 you should get about $3,609 annually assuming it will last thirty-five years and produce a 7% rate of return."

Bill's Age	Income Need	Pension Bill	Pension Bev	Total Income
55	$50,000	$3,609	$0	$3,609
56	$51,000	$3,609	$0	$3,609
57	$52,020	$3,609	$0	$3,609
58	$53,060	$3,609	$0	$3,609
59	$54,122	$3,609	$0	$3,609
60	$55,204	$3,609	$0	$3,609
61	$56,308	$3,609	$0	$3,609
62	$57,434	$3,609	$0	$3,609
63	$58,583	$3,609	$0	$3,609
64	$59,755	$3,609	$0	$3,609
65	$60,950	$3,609	$0	$3,609
70	$67,293	$3,609	$0	$3,609
75	$74,297	$3,609	$0	$3,609
80	$82,030	$3,609	$0	$3,609

SNAPSHOT AT AGE 55
CPP, OAS, RSP, DB Pension and DC Pension

Bill's Age	Income Need	Total Income	% of Need	Shortfall / Surplus
55	$50,000	$21,327	43%	($28,673)
56	$51,000	$21,537	42%	($29,463)
57	$52,020	$21,751	42%	($30,269)
58	$53,060	$21,970	41%	($31,090)
59	$54,122	$22,193	41%	($31,929)
60	$55,204	$29,851	54%	($25,353)
61	$56,308	$30,232	54%	($26,076)
62	$57,434	$30,619	53%	($26,815)
63	$58,583	$31,015	53%	($27,568)
64	$59,755	$31,419	53%	($28,336)
65	$60,950	$43,071	71%	($17,879)
70	$67,293	$53,190	79%	($14,103)
75	$74,297	$57,598	78%	($16,699)
80	$82,030	$62,466	76%	($19,564)
85	$90,568	$67,841	75%	($22,727)
90	$99,994	$73,776	74%	($26,218)

"You will notice that the amounts in the percentage of need column increase due to the inclusion of Old Age Security at age sixty-five. In addition, we assumed your RRSP and Defined Contribution pension plan monies were paid out at a level amount without indexing. Bill, we have one more source of income before we can see your total snapshot at age fifty-five."

"Is there anything else we need to know about Bill's DC pension plan?" asked Bev.

"There is no death benefit, no indexing, and no guarantee. Upon Bill's death, the remaining balance in the account goes to the beneficiaries. On a positive note, if you die early, these plans will provide more for the beneficiaries. These plans can work well but the employee must take charge of their future and plan for it. You need to understand that you are responsible for any shortfall and for fluctuations due to the markets or interest rates. That is absolutely critical to understand."

"What other source of income would that be? I thought this was all we had."

"You are right that there may not be any other sources today, but we should spend five minutes discussing the basic concepts in the event that your circumstances change in the future."

SUMMARY OF LEARNING

- DC pension plans define the employee contribution limits that are usually matched by the employer.

- The pension benefit is undefined and the employee is responsible for managing the investments and taking responsibility for their retirement income.

- Upon death, the beneficiaries receive the balance remaining in the account.

- DC plans are not guaranteed and you could outlive your money.

- Vesting entitles the employee to the employer's contributions.

NEXT CHAPTER

In chapter fourteen, discover the relevance of other sources of income which may already be taxed.

- 14 -

OTHER SOURCES OF INCOME

"Do you have any planned inheritance or any other source of non-registered money that should be included here?" Aunt Diggy asked.

"What do you mean by non-registered money?"

Diggy replied, "These are accounts that are not part of a registered plan like an RRSP or pension. They are typically completely open and not subject to rules like the registered plans and are much more flexible. Other sources of income in retirement could include income from part-time employment, the sale of a business, income from a rental property or other source that is not included elsewhere."

"My mother has a house and a little bit of money but we anticipate those funds will be required for healthcare so I do not plan on an inheritance."

"That is very wise and realistic of you Bill as I've seen many great intentions get changed due to increased health care costs or parents who decide to spend the money or give it to charity.

"What is very important to understand is that most other sources of income have already been taxed so their withdrawal is not subject to tax.

"For example, if your mother sells her house the proceeds will be tax-free since it is her principal residence. If she withdraws $10,000 of that principal each year from her account it will be tax-free. However, any earning on that money will be taxed. In comparison, if she were to take $10,000 out of an RRSP there would be tax to be paid since this would be included in her income. Other income can be very complicated so I won't cover it here but if you happen to have other non-registered sources of income then we will spend the time. CPP, OAS, Pension, RRSPs etc. are all taxable as income.

"Investments held outside an RRSP are taxed differently as can be seen in the following table:

Taxable Income	Interest Income	Capital Gains	Canadian Dividends
$0 - $32,183	22.05%	11.05%	4.49%
$32,184 - $32,435	28.05%	14.03%	11.98%
$32,436 - $57,111	31.15%	15.58%	15.86%
$57,112 - $64,368	32.98%	16.49%	16.86%
$64,369 - $64,870	36.98%	18.49%	23.67%
$64,871 - $67,289	39.39%	19.70%	27.59%
$67,290 - $104,648	43.41%	21.70%	27.59%
$104,649 +	46.41%	23.20%	31.34%

"You will notice that an individual who has a taxable income of $25,000 will pay 22% tax on interest income and only 11% for capital gains from stocks or property.

"In addition, capital gains are only taxable when realized, which means you don't pay on those paper gains until you sell, whereas interest income is taxable every year."

"Wow," said Bev. "You can really see the difference when you look at income sources from an after-tax perspective."

"We don't have much in non-registered accounts," said Bill, "but I appreciate you showing us that."

"Are you ready to see the final projected income snapshot at age fifty-five?"

"Yes, since you covered each of the income sources, inflation etc. I pretty well know exactly what to expect here. I would like a copy of the printout but now I want to know what things look like at age sixty-five when I really plan on retiring." Bill sounded like he knew exactly what he was talking about even though an hour ago he didn't have a clue about how much to expect or what to ask about his plan.

"Aunt Diggy, I want to say thank-you for spending all this time with us. I feel a lot better about these things now," said Bev warmly.

SUMMARY OF LEARNING

- Most other non-registered sources of income have already been taxed so they are not subject to tax upon withdrawal.

- Some other sources of income, like capital gains, are taxed at one half the rate of interest income.

- A principal residence can grow completely tax-free.

- Part-time work, inheritances and the sale of a business are all sources of other income.

NEXT CHAPTER

In chapter fifteen, put everything together to determine if Bev and Bill have enough to retire at age fifty-five.

INCOME AT AGE 55
(All sources included)

"Finally!" announced Aunt Diggy as she presented the final income snapshot at age fifty-five.

Bill's Age	Income Need	Total Income	% of Need	Shortfall / Surplus
55	$50,000	$21,327	43%	($28,673)
56	$51,000	$21,537	42%	($29,463)
57	$52,020	$21,751	42%	($30,269)
58	$53,060	$21,970	41%	($31,090)
59	$54,122	$22,193	41%	($31,929)
60	$55,204	$29,851	54%	($25,353)
61	$56,308	$30,232	54%	($26,076)
62	$57,434	$30,619	53%	($26,815)
63	$58,583	$31,015	53%	($27,568)
64	$59,755	$31,419	53%	($28,336)
65	$60,950	$43,071	71%	($17,879)
70	$67,293	$53,190	79%	($14,103)
75	$74,297	$57,598	78%	($16,699)
80	$82,030	$62,466	76%	($19,564)
85	$90,568	$67,841	75%	($22,727)
90	$99,994	$73,776	74%	($26,2180

"Here is your income snapshot at age fifty-five. It includes CPP, OAS, RRSP, DB and DC pension plans. Can you base any conclusions on this?"

"Yes, those guys on the commercials must have won the lottery; retiring at fifty-five is unrealistic," said Bill.

Aunt Diggy said, "I have many clients who can retire at age fifty-five but they have been planning for years. I guess you will just have to work a little longer Bill. We know retirement at age fifty-five is not realistic in your case but what about age sixty-five?"

"I am now worried I will not have enough income at sixty-five. Can we go over those numbers please?"

"Of course, my program will only take a few minutes to change the numbers. You will be amazed at the difference ten years makes to a plan. Bev will still be a young 60-year-old or about thirty-nine American and Bill will be a full-fledged senior at age sixty-five and entitled to all the benefits like discounts and free coffee."

"Aunt Diggy, Bill really likes you or he would not listen to your jokes. Right Bill?"

"Yes dear. Retirement at age fifty-five would be okay if I did not eat for the first ten years and then lived on half of what I need for the rest of my life. I am really going to have to rethink my plans to retire."

"I know this is not great news but at least you know the importance of having a plan. Let's assume you continue to contribute $5,000 a year in your RRSP and let's see what another ten years will do. Don't be discouraged by the results. I know that money was used to buy the kids a new bike or take that memorable family vacation.

"Bill, let me ask you, was it important to go through this process and are you glad you did this *before* you retired rather than find out *after* you retired?"

"Aunt Diggy, Bev and I are truly grateful for all the work you have done. I don't know why I did not pay closer attention to this but I guess that commercial on TV prompted me to take action so I actually thank that company as well. This has truly been great and I know several family members who will be told about this experience so that they will not have unpleasant surprises.

"Now, let's look at the age sixty-five projection because I am getting a little worried about what my retirement might look like."

"Let's start with Canada Pension Plan and then work through the other sources. Since we have already covered the plan design and important questions it is really just a matter of recalculating the amounts which does not take any time at all when you have a computer program that does the work."

"Aunt Diggy, I want you to know that this has been a very informative session and we appreciate all the work you have done for us. I know the results didn't look good at age fifty-five but we needed to know this," said Bev.

SUMMARY OF LEARNING

- Retirement at age fifty-five is not realistic in Bill's case. His sources of income are designed to commence at age sixty-five and Bill has not planned properly for an early retirement.

- The retirement planning process with a certified financial planner has been invaluable. They have learned a lot in the two hours it took to prepare their plan. They might be disappointed with the results but are glad they went through this process before they retired.

NEXT CHAPTER

In chapter sixteen, see what Bill's retirement plan looks like at age sixty-five as compared to his plan at age fifty-five. Will he be able to retire or is he in for more surprises?

- 16 -

INCOME AT AGE 65

"Bill, if you recall our discussion of your CPP benefits at age fifty-five you had no benefits during your first five years and then from age sixty to sixty-five you had the option of taking a reduced pension.

"Yes, I remember all too well," he sighed.

"Bev, since you are five years younger than this old guy, you had to wait another five years after Bill before you could collect. During Bill's first ten years of retirement there would be no benefits for you."

"That's right," said Bev with a smile. "I'm five years younger than old Bill."

"I think you will both be pleasantly surprised at the difference waiting until sixty-five to retire makes versus the snapshot at age fifty-five."

Bill jumped in, "It has to be better or I'll have to work full-time during retirement to support us."

"Let's highlight some of the positive aspects of Canada Pension Plan at age sixty-five versus age fifty-five as follows:

1) Bill will receive benefits from day one rather than waiting five years for a reduced amount.

2) Bill's payments will not be reduced by 30%.

3) The benefit will be higher due to inflation and a longer contribution record.

4) Bev will immediately receive a reduced benefit at age sixty and has the option to wait five years to receive the full benefit at age sixty-five.

"To summarize, you will not see those five years at the start of your retirement with zero income from CPP and the additional five years after that with very low income from CPP since Bev is too young to collect. Would you like to see this in a chart like the age fifty-five?"

"Yes, I'm very interested in seeing the results," said Bill.

"The following chart will illustrate your income from CPP alone when Bill is age sixty-five."

Bill's Age	Income Need	CPP Bill	CPP Bev	Total Income
65	$60,950	$10,408	$3,642	$14,050
70	$67,293	$11,491	$4,022	$15,513
75	$74,297	$12,687	$4,440	$17,127
80	$82,030	$14,007	$4,902	$18,909
85	$90,568	$15,465	$5,413	$20,878
90	$99,994	$17,075	$5,976	$23,051

"The above picture looks really good but let's compare it to the overall need below:

Bill's Age	Income Need	Total Income	% of Need	Shortfall / Surplus
65	$60,950	$14,050	23%	($46,900)
70	$67,293	$15,513	23%	($51,780)
75	$74,297	$17,127	23%	($57,170)
80	$82,030	$18,909	23%	($63,121)
85	$90,568	$20,878	23%	($69,690)
90	$99,994	$23,051	23%	($76,943)

"Clearly, CPP will provide a more consistent stream of retirement income replacing about 23% of your income need from day one.

"However, Canada Pension Plan alone will not meet your goals even at age sixty-five so we will have to look at the other sources of income."

Aunt Diggy noticed that Bill had a great big smile and asked him why he was so happy.

Bill looked over at Bev and said, "I can't believe the difference a few years makes. Part of me is very happy that we now know this but the other part of me wonders how many people have no idea how these programs work and think they can retire at age fifty-five. I am so pleased that we came to see you and I am anxious to see the other sources at age sixty-five.

"I cannot wait to see the look on the faces of Duane, Pete and Brad when they see how much I know about retirement planning," joked Bill. "Aunt Diggy, I would like to invite you over to the house next Saturday to join us for some of my famous chilli and to watch the game with my buddies."

"I am honoured that you would ask Bill. Of course, I will join you," replied Aunt Diggy.

OLD AGE SECURITY AT AGE 65

"Let us recap what OAS pension looked like for your age fifty-five retirement."

Bill interrupted and said, "Allow me as this is real simple. Since OAS only kicks in at age sixty-five I would get a big fat zero for the first ten years until age sixty-five and Bev would get a big fat zero for the first fifteen years. I'll probably be dead before we collect any substantial amount!"

"That's a little more blunt than I would put it but you have got the facts correct," said Aunt Diggy.

Aunt Diggy noticed that Bev was quiet but had a smile on her face and asked her if she had anything to say.

Bev smiled and said, "I am just sitting back and enjoying this. Watching Bill's expression about how little he has at fifty-five and how much he has at age sixty-five is just priceless. His comments make me laugh. I just know he is going to go to his buddies on Saturday night to prove how smart he is and is going to make them believe he has known this stuff for years."

Bill was silent with a boyish smirk on his face because he knew Bev was absolutely right.

"Let's summarize what you will get from OAS at age sixty-five Bill:

1) Full benefits start from day one so no waiting ten years for the benefit.

2) Bev will still have to wait five years to receive her first cheque but that is better than fifteen years.

3) Payment amounts will be equal because it is based on residency. Unlike CPP that penalized Bev for

lower contributions, the OAS program will provide the full benefit.

4) Payments are fully indexed for inflation and are payable for your lifetime.

5) The OAS clawback does not apply at your income level so you keep all the payments."

Bev commented this time, "It is about time that men and women received the same benefits from the government. I like the OAS system but wish they had the option of taking it at age sixty with a reduced amount to smooth out the income."

"We assume the annual benefit from OAS at age sixty-five will be $6,631. This is the current maximum indexed at 2% for inflation. "Here is the projected benefit from OAS alone."

Bill's Age	Income Need	OAS Bill	OAS Bev	Total Income
65	$60,950	$6,631	0	$6,631
70	$67,293	$7,322	$7,322	$14,644
75	$74,297	$8,084	$8,084	$16,168
80	$82,030	$8,925	$8,925	$17,850
85	$90,568	$9,854	$9,854	$19,708
90	$99,994	$10,879	$10,879	$21,758

"In the first five years the income is lower because Bev will not be eligible until she is sixty-five. However, once Bill is seventy and Bev is sixty-five you will both be eligible for the maximum benefits. The chart assumes the payments will increase by 2% each year in line with the assumed increase in the cost of goods and services.

"The following table will display your position at age sixty-five including just the government programs of CPP and OAS."

Bill's Age	Income Need	Total Income	% of Need	Shortfall / Surplus
65	$60,950	$20,681	34%	($40,269)
70	$67,293	$30,157	45%	($37,136)
75	$74,297	$33,295	45%	($41,002)
80	$82,030	$36,759	45%	($45,271)
85	$90,568	$40,586	45%	($49,982)
90	$99,994	$44,809	45%	($55,185)

"Not too shabby," said Bill. "This certainly isn't going to make me rich but I'm not going to starve either."

Bev looked at Bill, "I do not think we have to worry about you starving for quite some time," and then laughed.

Bill said, "Let's move on to my pension plan as I am sure there will be more good news."

Aunt Diggy commented, "Retirement at age fifty-five is realistic if you get good trusted advice and have a solid plan where you take action. Expecting to retire at age fifty-five without having even thought about it to age fifty-five is not realistic. If anything, those commercials got you to come see me so there is tremendous value in them in terms of creating awareness."

RRSPs AT AGE 65

"More good news here Bill. First, at age fifty-five you had $100,000 in your RRSP that had to last an estimated thirty-five years to age ninety. Keeping it simple with a level payment that doesn't increase with inflation you would get approximately $7,218 with the money running out in your ninetieth year assuming a 7% rate of return.

"The first good news is that $100,000 invested at 7% will double in ten years so at age sixty-five you should have about $200,000 without contributions."

"Wow," said Bill, "maybe I should retire at age seventy-five and buy a yacht and a beachfront condo like that guy on TV."

"The second piece of good news is your money only needs to last about twenty-five years from age sixty-five to ninety so about 50% less time for payments. Just as CPP reduces your amount for taking the payment earlier for more years, the reverse is true here. So your payments will substantially increase due to the shorter collection period.

"Do you want to guess how much you will receive Bill?"

"No, the last time that cost me dinner for two at Vidalia's Place."

"Come on," said Bev, "Aunt Diggy has just provided you with all the clues so this should be easy."

"Okay, I think it will increase the payments to $15,000 a year rather than the $7,218."

Bev said, "If it is less, I'll cook for your buddies for the playoffs every night during the final series and if you lose, we take that shopping weekend to the States and you cannot complain once about shopping all day. In fact, I will try not to remind you to factor in the exchange each time you find something that you think is a deal."

"Those are pretty high stakes but come to think of it barbecued steaks would be nice this time of year," said Bill. "It is a bet. How can I lose? If the amount is higher then I win and if the amount is lower I win."

With great anticipation they waited for Aunt Diggy to provide the answer. "Bev, you realize that Bill has increased the amount substantially and has learned a lot, which should help come in handy in getting the best bargains when you go for your shopping weekend," said Aunt Diggy with a roaring laugh. Bev thought that was just hilarious.

Bill couldn't believe it. "How much am I going to get?"

"How does $16,000 a year sound?"

Bill was shocked. On the one hand he lost the bet but knowing that his payments would double he generously said that they would stay in a real hotel and go to real restaurants during their trip. Both Bev and Bill were very happy.

"Bill, you will not be getting $16,000 a year from your RRSPs."

"But I thought you said it would be double because of the growth to $200,000 and the time required is now twenty-five years instead of thirty-five years. I can see the $16,000 right here on the chart."

"Yes, the $200,000 will provide about $16,000 a year but you forgot about the contributions you have been making and how much they will grow. You won't have $200,000, you will have about $270,000 so if you look at the chart you will get about $21,000 a year."

Bill was very pleased with this knowledge. "This is almost as good as the Leafs beating the Habs."

"The following chart will show the RRSP income

assuming a level payment at age sixty-five with the funds totally depleted by the time Bill is age ninety. $100,000 @ 7% plus $5,000 year = $270,633. Equal payment at 7% for 25 years = $21,704."

Bill's Age	Income Need	RRSP Bill	RRSP Bev	Total Income
65	$60,950	$21,704	$0	$21,704
70	$67,293	$21,704	$0	$21,704
75	$74,297	$21,704	$0	$21,704
80	$82,030	$21,704	$0	$21,704
85	$90,568	$21,704	$0	$21,704
90	$99,994	$21,704	$0	$21,704

"It is important to note that OAS and CPP are payable for life and fully indexed for inflation whereas your RRSP projections are expected to run out at age ninety and are a level payment."

"Why is that?" asked Bev.

"This is just a projection and it is a lot easier to show a level payment.

"I like your approach," said Bev. "This is reasonable so thanks for explaining it."

Bill said, "I agree that this is reasonable. I like the idea of some of my income being guaranteed for life and indexed for inflation and some of it with the RRSPs to have some flexibility to take a little more or a little less if I want."

"Let's put it all together so far showing the chart with CPP, OAS and RRSPs at Bill's age sixty-five."

Bill's Age	Income Need	Total Income	% of Need	Shortfall / Surplus
65	$60,950	$42,385	70%	($18,565)
70	$67,293	$51,861	77%	($15,432)
75	$74,297	$54,999	74%	($19,298)
80	$82,030	$58,463	71%	($23,567)
85	$90,568	$62,290	69%	($28,278)
90	$99,994	$66,513	67%	($33,4810

"Bill it appears you will have a little bit more than 70% of your need in retirement without including your pension plans. Let's move on to pensions."

"Now, where were we? Oh yes. Bill has accumulated another ten years of service and is no longer subject to a reduced pension. His income has also increased 2% annually during those five years. What amount will Bill now receive and how does this compare to what he projected at age fifty-five? If you thought the CPP, OAS and RRSP are great at age sixty-five versus age fifty-five you will really like your pension plan.

"First, you will now have thirty-five years of service and at 1% per year it will be 35% of your income versus 25% at age fifty-five. Two, your average income level will be higher which translates into higher benefits.

"Three, no reduced penalty because you are sixty-five. Plus you get a gold watch for thirty-five years of service."

"That sounds just wonderful," said Bill enthusiastically. "I'm enjoying this very much."

"Income increases from $60,000 at age fifty-five to $83,000 at sixty-five. Hence, 35% = $29,050 per year. The following chart will show the income from your Defined Benefit pension plan. Notice that the amount of $29,050 is substantially higher than the $10,500 projected at age fifty-five."

"Yes, I noticed that," said Bill in a relaxed tone with a big smile on his face.

Bill's Age	Income Need	DB Bill	DB Bev	Total Income
65	$60,950	$29,050	$0	$29,050
70	$67,293	$31,445	$0	$31,445
75	$74,297	$34,717	$0	$34,717
80	$82,030	$38,331	$0	$38,331
85	$90,568	$42,320	$0	$42,320
90	$99,994	$46,725	$0	$46,725

TOTAL INCOME SNAPSHOT AT AGE 65
(OAS, CPP, RRSP, DB pension plan)

Bill's Age	Income Need	Total Income	% of Need	Shortfall / Surplus
65	$60,950	$71,435	117%	+$10,485
70	$67,293	$83,306	124%	+$16,013
75	$74,297	$89,716	121%	+$15,419
80	$82,030	$96,794	118%	+$14,764
85	$90,568	$104,610	116%	+$14,042
90	$99,994	$113,238	113%	+$13,244

"Your income at age sixty-five will significantly exceed your income requirements."

"I still cannot get over what a difference ten years makes to a plan," said Bill shaking his head. "It is very interesting how the age fifty-five projection is so much lower than I had thought and the age sixty-five projection is much higher than I had anticipated."

Bev interjected, "It just goes to show how little we know about retirement planning and how much value Aunt Diggy has provided to us. We thank you for that."

"Just like the RRSP the value increases but in addition you receive an additional 10 years of employer contributions. And just like the RRSP you had thirty-five years of collecting now it is twenty-five years."

"I will have so much cash I will not know what to do with it," joked Bill.

"The key is that you will be ahead of your projection at sixty-five and significantly below at fifty-five. We can fool around with the numbers to get the exact age but if you are comfortable with age sixty-five we can reassess this each year as part of an annual review.

"$50,000 at 7% plus $1,600 a year increased by 3% each year = $125,000. Investing this at 7% for 25 years produces $10,025 so let's say $10,000 annually which is about triple what you would get at age fifty-five."

Bill's Age	Income Need	DC Bill	DC Bev	Total / Income
55	$50,000	$10,000	$0	$10,000
65	$60,950	$10,000	$0	$10,000
70	$67,293	$10,000	$0	$10,000
75	$74,297	$10,000	$0	$10,000
80	$82,030	$10,000	$0	$10,000
85	$90,568	$10,000	$0	$10,000
90	$99,994	$10,000	$0	$10,000

FINAL SNAPSHOT (TOTAL INCOME AT AGE 65)

Bill's Age	Income Need	Total Income	% of Need	Shortfall / Surplus
65	$60,950	$81,435	134%	+$20,485
70	$67,293	$93,306	139%	+$26,013
75	$74,297	$99,716	134%	+$25,419
80	$82,030	$106,794	130%	+$24,764
85	$90,568	$114,610	127%	+$24,042
90	$99,994	$123,238	123%	+$23,244

"What can I say folks that is not already obvious in the chart? Let's compare the original income projections at age fifty-five versus age sixty-five. It is so different it is almost unbelievable. Now are you glad you came in to see me?"

"Absolutely, so what do we owe you? This was well worth the time," said Bill.

"Absolutely nothing. I would like the opportunity to manage your investments."

"You've got it," said Bev. "We have complete confidence in you."

"There is one thing you can do, and that is to help a friend."

"How so?" asked Bill.

"Here are my business cards. If you can give them to a friend and tell them about your experience you will be helping them out and I will be successful because of the referrals. Just think how popular you will be with the guys."

"Here are three names right now: Brad, Duane and Pete. You can meet them at our home on Saturday night."

Aunt Diggy gave them a big hug and said, "Don't forget to tell your kids you love them."

Then Bill announced, "I am so impressed that I'm taking everyone out to the theatre and a nice dinner tonight. I arranged for Jenn to join us and she freed up your schedule so all four of us are going."

Bev had a loving smile and a tear in her eye, "Bill, that is one of the most thoughtful things you have ever done, and to surprise us."

"Aunt Diggy, I can't tell you how much this has meant to us. Sometimes I am a little stubborn but you have truly shown me the value in seeing a professional to talk about finances. I plan to move all my investments to you and will also refer my friends to you."

Bev gave Diggy a big hug and thanked her for everything. Bill asked if he could have a few cookies to go and Jenn had already boxed up some of their favourites for them both.

"Remember that a plan is only as good as the action you take to implement it and it must be reviewed on an annual basis," Diggy said as they got their jackets.

SUMMARY OF LEARNING

- Income goes from a significant shortfall at age fifty-five to an excess of income at age sixty-five.

- The shortfall is primarily due to CPP, OAS and company pension plans that are designed to commence at age sixty-five without penalty versus age fifty-five with a reduced amount.

- In addition, the extra ten years of growth on the investments and ten fewer years on drawing income in retirement will significantly increase the income in retirement at age sixty-five.

NEXT CHAPTER

In chapter seventeen, the conclusion will wrap up the book and summarize the learning. What will Aunt Diggy have to say?

- 17 -

CONCLUSION

Retirement planning is more than just numbers; it really comes down to balancing your lifestyle today and your lifestyle in the future.

You should establish realistic goals and objectives and seek the advice of a certified financial planner to put a plan in place. There is no right or wrong answer but it is absolutely essential that you verify the accuracy of your plan.

Early retirement at age fifty-five is possible but get the facts of your income stream and know the important questions to ask. Clearly Aunt Diggy helped Bev and Bill realize that retirement at age fifty-five isn't realistic in their case and age sixty-five is very good. They will take action on the recommendations and meet for an annual review, or when significant events occur, to ensure they are on track.

A week later they were watching TV and Bill said, "Come here Bev and see this commercial." Bev and Bill just smiled at each other and said, "Thanks Aunt Diggy."

Look for more Aunt Diggy guides soon, including...

- *Aunt Diggy's Guide to RRIFs and Annuities*

- *Aunt Diggy's Guide to Investing*

- *Aunt Diggy's Guide to Life Insurance*

CONTACT THE AUTHOR

EMAIL: barrycarson@rogers.com
MAIL: Box 187, Delaware, Ontario N0L 1E0

- *Provide feedback to the author on this book or ideas for future publications.*

- *Arrange a no-cost, no-obligation initial meeting to discuss your personal finances.*

- *Order books - substantial discounts are available for bulk purchases.*

- *Arrange for the author to speak at your group meetings.*

- *Obtain media comments, quotes and interviews.*

- *Receive permission to quote passages.*

COMPOUND GROWTH ($1,000 LUMP SUM)

Years	5%	6%	7%	8%	9%
Start	$1,000	$1,000	$1,000	$1,000	$1,000
5	$1,276	$1,338	$1,403	$1,469	$1,539
10	$1,629	$1,791	$1,967	$2,159	$2,367
15	$2,079	$2,397	$2,759	$3,172	$3,642
20	$2,653	$3,207	$3,870	$4,661	$5,604
25	$3,386	$4,292	$5,427	$6,848	$8,623
30	$4,322	$5,743	$7,612	$10,063	$13,268
35	$5,516	$7,686	$10,677	$14,785	$20,414
40	$7,040	$10,286	$14,974	$21,725	$31,409
45	$8,985	$13,765	$21,002	$31,920	$48,327
50	$11,467	$18,420	$29,457	$46,902	$74,358
	11x	18x	29x	47x	74x

The power of compound interest is magical. Take note that the growth of $1,000 @ 5% over 50 years equals 11.5 times the original investment. Also note the difference between 5% and 9% growth over different time periods.

COMPOUND GROWTH ($100 / MONTH)

Years	5%	6%	7%	8%	9%
1	$1,232	$1,239	$1,245	$1,251	$1,258
5	$6,809	$6,982	$7,160	$7,341	$7,527
10	$15,499	$16,326	$17,202	$18,128	$19,109
15	$26,590	$28,831	$31,286	$33,978	$36,928
20	$40,746	$45,565	$51,041	$57,266	$64,346
25	$58,812	$67,958	$78,747	$91,484	$106,531
30	$81,870	$97,926	$117,606	$141,761	$171,438
35	$111,298	$138,029	$172,109	$215,635	$271,306
40	$148,856	$191,696	$248,552	$324,180	$424,965
45	$196,792	$263,515	$355,766	$483,669	$661,388
50	$257,971	$359,625	$506,141	$718,009	$1,025,155

See the dramatic growth of just $100/month over different time periods and different interest rates. $100/month at 9% over 50 years will be worth more than $1,000,000. Even if inflation were at 5%, this amount ($1,025,155) is still $750,000 ahead of the game after inflation ($257,971).

CANADA PENSION PLAN 2004

Starting Age	Maximum "Monthly" Benefit	% of Normal Amount at age 65	Maximum "Annual" Benefit
60	$489	70%	$5,862
61	$619	76%	$7,425
62	$668	82%	$8,011
63	$716	88%	$8,598
64	$765	94%	$9,184
65	$814	100%	$9,770
66	$863	106%	$10,356
67	$912	112%	$10,942
68	$961	118%	$11,529
69	$1,010	124%	$12,115
70	$1,058	130%	$12,701

www.hrdc-drhc.gc.ca/isp 1-800 277-9914

- Pension taken *before* age 65 is *reduced* by (6% year)
- Pension taken *after* age 65 is *increased* by (6% year)
- Payable for life and fully indexed for inflation

OLD AGE SECURITY 2004

Effective January 1, 2004

Individual Net Income	Annual Clawback	Annual Benefit	Monthly Benefit
$59,790	$0	$5,550	$462
$60,000	$31	$5,519	$460
$65,000	$781	$4,769	$397
$70,000	$1,531	$4,019	$335
$75,000	$2,281	$3,269	$272
$80,000	$3,031	$2,519	$210
$85,000	$3,781	$1,769	$147
$90,000	$4,531	$1,019	$85
$96,788	$5,550	$0	$0

A: Individual Net Income	$80,000	A
B: Subtract OAS Threshold	- $59,790	B
C: Income Subject to Clawback	= $20,210	C
D: Box "C" x 15% = Clawback	$3,031	D
E: *Annual* Benefit $5,350 - "D"	$2,519	E
F: *Monthly* Benefit = "E" / .12	$210	F

HISTORICAL RATES OF RETURN

As at September 30, 2003
Average compound returns (after management fees)
Source: Globe Hysales

Fund Category	1 YR	3 YR	5 YR	10 YR
Inflation (CPI)	4.3	2.7	2.4	1.8
1-year GICs	1.6	3.0	3.3	4.0
5-year GICs	4.0	4.5	4.6	5.5
Canadian Equity	(13.5)	(2.2)	2.0	8.8
Canadian Bond	6.5	6.9	4.9	7.1
Canadian Balanced	(6.0)	0.0	2.5	7.5
U.S. Equity (Canadian $)	(24.8)	(15.1)	(2.3)	7.1
Global Equity (Canadian $)	(20.7)	(14.0)	(1.4)	6.6

Fund Category	2003	2002	2001	2000
Inflation (CPI)	4.3	0.7	3.2	2.6
1-year GICs	1.6	2.7	4.8	3.9
5-year GICs	4.0	4.1	5.5	4.9
Canadian Equity	(13.5)	(4.0)	12.6	20.4
Canadian Bond	6.5	5.8	8.3	(2.8)
Canadian Balanced	(6.0)	(0.9)	7.7	8.4
U.S. Equity (Canadian $)	(24.8)	(10.3)	(8.0)	13.2
Global Equity (Canadian $)	(20.7)	(12.7)	(6.5)	22.6

MINIMUM RRIF WITHDRAWALS
(AGES 50-69)

Age January 1st	Minimum %	Minimum $100,000 Balance
50	2.50%	$2,500
51	2.56%	$2,560
52	2.63%	$2,630
53	2.70%	$2,700
54	2.78%	$2,780
55	2.86%	$2,860
56	2.94%	$2,940
57	3.03%	$3,030
58	3.13%	$3,130
59	3.23%	$3,230
60	3.33%	$3,330
61	3.45%	$3,450
62	3.57%	$3,570
63	3.70%	$3,700
64	3.85%	$3,850
65	4.00%	$4,000
66	4.17%	$4,170
67	4.35%	$4,350
68	4.55%	$4,550
69	4.76%	$4,760

- Can be based on age of younger spouse
- RSP to RRIF conversion not required until December 31 of your 69th year

MINIMUM RRIF WITHDRAWALS
(AGE 70-94+)

Age Jan 1st	Minimum %	Minimum *Annual* $100,000 Balance	Minimum *Monthly* $100,000 Balance
70	5.00%	$5,000	$416.67
71	7.38%	$7,380	$615.00
72	7.48%	$7,480	$623.33
73	7.59%	$7,590	$632.50
74	7.71%	$7,710	$642.50
75	7.85%	$7,850	$654.17
76	7.99%	$7,990	$665.83
77	8.15%	$8,150	$679.17
78	8.33%	$8,330	$694.17
79	8.53%	$8,530	$710.83
80	8.75%	$8,750	$729.17
81	8.99%	$8,990	$749.17
82	9.27%	$9,270	$772.50
83	9.58%	$9,580	$798.33
84	9.93%	$9,930	$827.50
85	10.33%	$10,330	$860.83
86	10.79%	$10,790	$899.17
87	11.33%	$11,330	$944.17
88	11.96%	$11,960	$996.67
89	12.71%	$12,710	$1,059.17
90	13.62%	$13,620	$1,135.00
91	14.73%	$14,730	$1,227.50
92	16.12%	$16,120	$1,343.33
93	17.92%	$17,920	$1,493.33
94+	20.00%	$20,000	$1,666.67

LIFE INCOME FUND (LIF) - WITHDRAWALS

Age	Minimum %	Maximum %	Minimum $100,000	Maximum $100,000
55	2.86%	6.51%	$2,860	$6,510
56	2.94%	6.57%	$2,940	$6,570
57	3.03%	6.63%	$3,030	$6,630
58	3.13%	6.70%	$3,130	$6,700
59	3.23%	6.77%	$3,230	$6,770
60	3.33%	6.85%	$3,330	$6,850
61	3.45%	6.94%	$3,450	$6,940
62	3.57%	7.04%	$3,570	$7,040
63	3.70%	7.14%	$3,700	$7,140
64	3.84%	7.26%	$3,840	$7,260
65	4.00%	7.38%	$4,000	$7,380
66	4.17%	7.52%	$4,170	$7,520
67	4.35%	7.67%	$4,350	$7,670
68	4.55%	7.83%	$4,550	$7,830
69	4.76%	8.02%	$4,760	$8,020
70	5.00%	8.22%	$5,000	$8,220
71	7.38%	8.45%	$7,380	$8,450
72	7.48%	8.71%	$7,480	$8,710
73	7.59%	9.00%	$7,590	$9,000
74	7.71%	9.34%	$7,710	$9,340
75	7.85%	9.71%	$7,850	$9,710
76	7.99%	10.15%	$7,990	$10,150
77	8.15%	10.66%	$8,150	$10,660
78	8.33%	11.25%	$8,330	$11,250
79*	8.53%	11.96%	$8,530	$11,960

*Annuity must be purchased at age 80

WEBSITES

Human Resources Development Canada (CPP / OAS)	www.hrdc-drhc.gc.ca/isp	1-800-277-9914
Canada Customs and Revenue Agency (Taxation)	www.ccra-adrc.gc.ca	1-800-267-3395
Financial Services Commission of Ontario (Pensions)	www.fsco.gov.on.ca	1-800-668-0128
Securities Commission (Regulatory)	www.osc.gov.on.ca	1-877-785-1555
Stevenson & Hunt Insurance & Investment Brokers	www.sthunt.com	1-519-963-3558

NOTES

NOTES

NOTES

NOTES

NOTES

NOTES

NOTES

NOTES

NOTES

NOTES

NOTES

NOTES

NOTES